The Gospels in Current Study

The Gospels in Current Study

Second Edition

Simon J. Kistemaker

BAKER BOOK HOUSE
Grand Rapids, Michigan

Copyright 1972 by
Baker Book House Company
ISBN: 0-8010-5316-1

Library of Congress Catalog Card Number: 72-78255

Second Edition issued October 1980

Second printing, August 1986

PHOTOLITHOPRINTED BY CUSHING - MALLOY, INC.
ANN ARBOR, MICHIGAN, UNITED STATES OF AMERICA

CONTENTS

PREFACE

What is going on in the field of New Testament studies? This question is repeatedly asked by theologian and layman, by preacher and student. When we voice the question, we reveal a number of things; for example, we are interested in studies of the New Testament, but we are unable to keep up with the flood of literature because we do not have the time.

We have time, however, to read summaries of studies in the area of the New Testament. Precisely for this reason, I have set about to write a book which surveys, condenses, and to a degree, popularizes these studies.

A survey of all New Testament studies would be too extensive and would result in an impressive volume. Therefore, I have summarized only those studies pertaining to the Gospels. It has not been my aim to present an exhaustive and complete compendium; rather, this book intends to be a readable and informative survey of recent Gospel studies. In short, this survey gives the reader a nodding acquaintance with and an ability to speak intelligently about these studies.

Another reason for writing this book is time itself. More than a quarter of a century has passed since the discoveries of the Gospel of Thomas and the Dead Sea Scrolls. Also, during the last two decades, the gospel has been reinterpreted by leading form critics, the history of Jesus has been reexamined, and redaction criticism has appeared among the disciplines of New Testament studies. The time has come to take inventory, to assess the pursuits of New Testament theologians, to evaluate their criticism and interpretation of the Gospels, and to test their theology on the touchstone of Scripture.

By writing a survey which is both scholarly and popular, I take the risk of incurring the accusation from the theologian that this work is not scholarly enough and from the general reader that it could have been more popular. I trust, however, that the purpose of this book is fully justified. For inaccuracies, whatever they may be, I take full responsibility and offer my apologies.

May the Lord Jesus Christ, whose resurrection from the dead we celebrate, be pleased to bless this book to the glory and honor of God the Father.

Simon J. Kistemaker

Easter 1972
Jackson, Mississippi

PREFACE TO THE SECOND EDITION

Since the first printing of this book, we have seen the further development of studies of the Gospels. I have tried to give expression to some of the changes, particularly where they touch on the interpretation of the Biblical text, in the final chapter of this edition.

The second edition has provided an opportunity to correct inaccuracies which appeared in the first printing and to amplify and update the bibliography.

The reception which this book has received thus far has been a tremendous source of satisfaction to me. May the Lord continue to bless the efforts put forth to acquaint the reader with current studies in the Gospels.

Simon J. Kistemaker

Summer 1980
Jackson, Mississippi

1. MANUSCRIPTS

I. GOSPEL OF THOMAS

History

Even though the publication of the Gospel of Thomas in 1958 caused the British press to call it the "fifth Gospel," after the sensational dimension of this recently discovered gospel had disappeared, the average reader knew that another apocryphal gospel had come to light.

Before this gospel was discovered in the sands of Egypt, at least three papyri leaves had been unearthed in a place called Oxyrhynchus (now known as Behnesa) some one hundred miles south of Cairo, Egypt. In 1897, two British scholars, B. P. Grenfell and A. S. Hunt, found among some early Christian literature a papyrus leaf written in Greek. This leaf which dates from about A.D. 200 contained seven sayings of Jesus which had this in common, that every saying is introduced by "Jesus said." In other words, the leaf gave evidence of the fact that collections of Jesus-sayings circulated during the first few eras of Christianity.

Within another six years, in 1903, the same scholars, Grenfell and Hunt, discovered two more papyrus leaves at Oxyrhynchus similar to the one found earlier. One of the leaves contained six sayings of Jesus; the other, probably two. The condition of the two leaves was very poor so that the exact text could not be established. Yet one thing became increasingly clear to scholars: these papyrus leaves were traces of an unknown gospel.

More than forty years later this unknown gospel was unearthed by a few Egyptian fellahin who in search of fertilizer stumbled upon a library of some twelve volumes. In 1946, these laborers were in the little village of Nag-Hammadi located some 250 miles to the south of Cairo in a bend of the Nile. In earlier times, perhaps in the second and third centuries, a Gnostic religious group had gathered a library of Gnostic scriptures in the Coptic language. Among the twelve volumes which were preserved throughout the ages was the Gospel of Thomas, which in its beginning proved to be identical to the Greek fragments discovered by Grenfell and Hunt in 1897 and 1903.

The Gospel of Thomas, as far as the title was concerned, did not present itself as a newcomer, because its name had been known from the writings of the early Church Fathers. In the third century, both Hippolytus and Origen refer to the Gospel of Thomas. And upon further investigation, a word of Jesus quoted by Hippolytus from this gospel is identical to a saying of the gospel discovered at Nag-Hammadi.[1] Jesus said: "The man old in days will not hesitate to ask a little child of seven days about the place of Life, and he will live. For many who are first shall become last, and they shall become a single one" (Logion 4 in the Gospel of Thomas).

Though the title of the new document happens to be the Gospel of Thomas, the work is not a gospel at all. After the introductory words: "These are the secret words which Jesus the Living spoke and which Didymus Judas Thomas wrote," some 114 sayings follow, most of which are introduced by "Jesus said," or "He said," or "Jesus said to his disciples." At times, the disciples ask a question, which later is answered by Jesus. Even women ask questions; both Mary and Salome quiz Jesus.

Apart from these individual sayings of Jesus, the gospel does not have a birth narrative, not even an account of Jesus' life, death, and resurrection. It contains merely sayings and parables, many of which are identical to those in the canonical Gospels. Yet the wording of those sayings which are identical is not exact. The sayings in the Gospel of Thomas do not preserve an authentic tradition of the words of Jesus parallel to those in the canonical Gospels. Rather, they are dependent upon the canonical Gospels. In fact, they serve to advance the cause of Gnosticism to a large extent.

This raises the question: When was the gospel written? If Hippolytus and Origen knew the gospel and even quoted it, the third century can be regarded as the time in which the gospel freely circulated. Undoubtedly, the original goes back to the second century, especially since a certain parallelism has been ascertained between the Gospel of Thomas and the Diatessaron of Tatian written about A.D. 175.[2]

Absolute certainty in pinpointing the date of the Gospel of Thomas cannot be attained, for the possibility exists that Thomas' Gospel and

---

[1]E. Hennecke, W. Schneemelcher, *New Testament Apocrypha*. Vol. I, Philadelphia: Westminster, 1959; pp. 283f.

[2]G. Quispel, "L'Evangile selon Thomas et le Diatessaron." *Vigiliae Christianae* 13 (1959); pp. 87ff.

Tatian's Diatessaron go back to an earlier document. Generally, however, the Gospel of Thomas is said to stem from the second century.

Relation to the New Testament

Because of this relatively late dating of the Gospel of Thomas, this gospel does not contribute much to a better understanding of the text of the canonical Gospels. Is there any value in studying this apocryphal gospel? Does it have any relation to the New Testament?

The answer to these questions is in the affirmative. Bertil Gärtner sketches the value of studying the 114 sayings (logia) of this gospel by saying, "The many logia in the *Gospel of Thomas* may be divided into three groups: first, those which reproduce sayings of Jesus which are preserved in the canonical Gospels; secondly, *agrapha* previously encountered, mainly in patristic literature; and thirdly, hitherto unknown sayings. Of these three groups, the first is by far the largest, in fact comprising about one-half of the 114 logia."[3] Detailed study of the text of the Gospel of Thomas has revealed that the source for this gospel is not a tradition independent from the canonical Gospels, but that it is really dependent on the canonical Gospels. Yet the fact remains that the collection of Jesus-sayings points to a practice in the first two centuries, during which such collections were derived from oral tradition.

Moreover, the discovery of the Gospel of Thomas has proved the existence of sayings collected in the form of an anthology or testimony book. "One argument which could be brought against the hypothesis of a sayings-source was that no document consisting solely of sayings was known to have existed. With the discovery of Thomas this argument, of course, falls; but this fact makes it necessary to guard against the hasty conclusion that in Thomas we have either the long-lost Q, whether or not it was identical with the *logia* mentioned by Papias, or a form of Q."[4] In all probability, the author of the Gospel of Thomas wanted to give his readers the impression that they were in possession of "secret words" which Jesus the Living one had spoken.[5]

The sayings in the Gospel of Thomas which do not have a parallel in the canonical Gospels either support the sayings of Jesus recorded in patristic literature or give evidence of sayings of Jesus thus far unknown. Nevertheless, these unknown sayings which the Gospel of Thomas reveals may have been changed considerably within the Gnostic environment in which it originated. Therefore the genuineness of these sayings of Jesus has been invalidated.

---

[3]*The Theology of the Gospel of Thomas.* New York: Harper & Brothers, 1961; p. 44.
[4]R. McL. Wilson, *Studies in the Gospel of Thomas.* London: Mowbray, 1960; pp. 45f.
[5]R. M. Grant, *The Secret Sayings of Jesus.* New York: Doubleday, 1960; p. 109.

What then is the significance of this collection of sayings? R. McL. Wilson sees its primary significance in the light which the Gospel of Thomas sheds upon Gnosticism, in view of the scarcity of original documents of the Gnostic sect.[6] And a document which provides information about the teaching and influence of a sect which, in the last part of the first century and certainly throughout the second, undermined Christianity is a worthy and welcome addition to the store of New Testament knowledge.

II. DEAD SEA SCROLLS

Survey

Little did Muhammad the Wolf, a Bedouin goatherd, realize that he had come upon a treasure much more valuable than gold. In the spring of 1947 — some say 1945 — he playfully threw a rock into the circular opening of a cave along the northwest edge of the Dead Sea and heard the sound of a breaking jar. When he returned the next day accompanied by a friend, they both squeezed through the narrow opening of the cave and explored the inside, hoping to discover untold riches in gold. They found, however, no gold but a number of large jars which contained scrolls made of brown leather. And upon the scrolls, letters were written which were unknown to them. Evidently they saw some value in taking the scrolls along, and when they came to Bethlehem, some time afterward, they sold three scrolls on the black market. Finally, after the scrolls had changed hands a few times, they were examined by the late Eleazar L. Sukenik, Professor of Archaeology at the Hebrew University. He then made contact with the American School of Oriental Research where scholars provisionally dated the scrolls between 200 B.C. and A.D. 100. Eventually, the scrolls were purchased by Dr. Sukenik and his son and placed by the Israeli Government in a museum called "The Shrine of the Books," located in the city of Jerusalem.

All told, Dr. Sukenik and his son, General Yigael Yadin, bought seven scrolls which came out of the cave discovered by the Bedouin goatherd. They are successively: a complete scroll of Isaiah, written in Hebrew and apart from a few words is exactly the same as the Book of Isaiah in the Hebrew Bible; next, a scroll which lists the rules and regulations of the people who had stored these scrolls —this scroll is known as the *Manual of Discipline;* the third scroll is a commentary on the Book of Habakkuk; the fourth, written in Aramaic, contains the apocryphal account of some patriarchs of Genesis, and is called the

---

[6]*Op. cit.,* p. 151.

Genesis Apocryphon; the fifth is an incomplete scroll of Isaiah, which bears the name the *Hebrew University Isaiah Scroll;* the sixth scroll is the so-called *War Scroll;* and the last, because of its thirty hymns resembling the Psalms, bears the title *Thanksgiving Hymns.*

Once the source of the scrolls was determined and permission granted to excavate the area known as Qumran, more than three hundred caves were explored, though only eleven caves contained scrolls and fragments of manuscripts. These eleven were given numbers, so that the cave discovered by Muhammad the Wolf has the distinction of being Cave 1. And of these eleven, only Caves 1, 4, and 11 produced scrolls of Biblical writings. About four hundred different manuscripts have been discovered which range from ten scrolls with complete text to numerous fragments of limited value. "Every book of the Hebrew Bible, except the Book of Esther, is represented in the Qumran finds. The Book of Esther fails to appear, while parts of books such as Deuteronomy, Isaiah, or the Minor Prophets and the Psalms are represented by more than ten copies."[7]

At first, a simple system was devised to designate the manuscripts by some convenient abbreviation in English. The Dead Sea Scrolls became known as the DSS, and the two Isaiah scrolls as DSI^a and DSI^b. But when discoveries were made in the several caves near Qumran and near Wady Murabba'at, a new system of designating manuscripts became imperative. Thus the letter Q now stands for Qumran, the letter M for Murabba'at. The caves also received a number: discoveries of Cave 1 at Qumran are labelled 1Q, those of Cave 4 as 4Q. No longer is the English name of the scroll abbreviated, but the Hebrew name. The Manual of Discipline is abbreviated as 1QS. The complete Isaiah scroll, known in English as Isaiah A, has been given the new abbreviation $1QIsa^a$ and the second Isaiah scroll, Isaiah B, has become $1QIsa^b$. The Habakkuk Commentary has the abbreviation 1QpHab; the letter p stands for the Aramaic word *pesher,* which means commentary. Likewise, the Nahum commentary, discovered in Cave 4 has been designated 4QpNah. The only manuscript that retained its original name in the abbreviation is the Genesis Apocryphon, now known as $1QGen^{apoc}$. This new system of reference is the accepted norm.

Religious Community

Who put these scrolls in caves? Who wrote them?

These questions were soon answered when archaeologists began to excavate ancient ruins situated not even one-eighth mile east of Cave 1. The main ruin is known as Khirbet Qumran with a second ruin about

---

[7]M. Mansoor, *The Dead Sea Scrolls.* Grand Rapids: Eerdmans, 1964; p. 6.

three miles south. These ruins, when excavated, turned out to be a monastery in which a religious community had lived from the second century B.C. to A.D. 68. This religious community wrote and copied the manuscripts discovered in the eleven caves.

Who were these people who made up the religious community during that particular time in history? The manuscripts themselves do not mention the religious community by name. But the evidence which comes from the writings of the Elder Pliny, Philo, and Josephus points to the Essenes, a Jewish sect which lived at the Qumran monastery during the time of Christ. Josephus describes the three branches of Jewish religion during that time by speaking of Pharisees, Sadducees, and Essenes. The New Testament relates information about the first two branches but is silent about the third. Thus, who were the Essenes?

Their Greek name *Essenes* goes back to Jewish Palestinian Aramaic speech. This Greek word may very well have been a popular name given to these people but which was never used by them; it never occurs in the manuscripts found at Qumran![8] In Aramaic, the word is *hasayya* which finds its equivalent in the Hebrew *hasidim;* these terms have the meaning "pious" or "holy." In short, the Essenes were the holy ones among the Jewish people. "It is generally believed that the Essenes made their first appearance during or toward the end of the Maccabean revolt, in the second century B.C., when the priesthood under Sadduceeism was in its lowest repute, especially because of its close association with Hellenism."[9] These Essenes generally lived in monasteries to keep themselves unspotted from the defilements of the world around them.

The relation between the Essenes and the New Testament becomes significant when the life of John the Baptist is considered. John lived in the wilderness of Judea, where he later preached and baptized the people in the river Jordan. He lived and worked within a few miles of the Essene community of Qumran whose ascetic characteristics he shared. It is not out of the question that John the Baptist was acquainted with the Essenes and was possibly influenced by them. In his divine commission, however, he knew, served, and proclaimed the true Messiah.

Bearing on the New Testament

What bearing do the Dead Sea Scrolls have on the New Testament? The relationships between these two bodies of literature usually con-

---

[8]M. Black, *The Scrolls and Christian Origins.* New York: Charles Scribner's Sons, 1961; p. 14.

[9]Mansoor, *op. cit.,* p. 125.

verge on the life of John the Baptist, the Gospel and Epistles of John, the Pauline Epistles, and the General Epistles.

The charter of the Qumran community was based on Isaiah 40:3, "In the wilderness prepare the way of the Lord; make straight in the desert a highway for our God" (1QS 8:13-15; 9:19-20). Yet this evidence, which immediately calls to mind the voice of the Baptist crying in the wilderness, cannot be regarded as the connecting link between the Essenes and John the Baptist. The members of the Qumran community were separatists who in their exclusion prepared themselves for the coming of the Kingdom of God.[10] John met the people at the river Jordan and told them to repent, for the Kingdom of Heaven is at hand (Matt. 3:2). For John, the way of the Lord had to be prepared by all people who repented of their sins and sought remission by being baptized.

Also, the Qumran community practiced baptism, yet the methods employed differed considerably. "It would appear that the Essenes practiced several washings, and that these were self-imposed, in contrast with the role of a baptizer in the rite of John."[11] Their washings were meant to cleanse the flesh which had come in contact with impurities; John's baptism was directed at inward cleansing of the heart which was performed by means of a single baptism.

The relationship between the Qumran scrolls and the Johannine writings is striking indeed. This is not to say that John depended upon the Dead Sea manuscripts in order to write his Gospel and Epistles, but the world out of which both the Essenes and the disciple of Jesus speak is the same. The fourth Gospel contains numerous phrases, references, and expressions found in the documents of Qumran. In some respects, parts of the Manual of Discipline "might be a commentary on parts of the first and eighth chapters of St. John's Gospel."[12]

> All that is and ever was comes from a God of knowledge. Before things came into existence He determined the plan of them; and when they fill their appointed roles, it is in accordance with His glorious design that they discharge their functions. Nothing can be changed. In His hand lies the government of all things. God it is that sustains them in their needs. Now, this God created man to rule the world, and appointed for him two spirits after whose direction he was to walk until the final Inquisition. They are the spirits of truth and perversity.
> The origin of truth lies in the Fountain of Light, and that of perversity in the Wellspring of Darkness. All who practice righteous-

---

[10]W. H. Brownlee, *The Meaning of the Qumran Scrolls for the Bible*. New York: Oxford University Press, 1964; p. 114.

[11]R. E. Murphy, *The Dead Sea Scrolls and the Bible*, Westminster, Maryland: Newman Press, 1963; p. 63.

[12]A. N. Gilkes, *The Impact of the Dead Sea Scrolls*. London: Macmillan, 1962; p. 154.

ness are under the domination of the Prince of Light, and walk in
ways of light; whereas all who practice perversity are under the
dominion of the Angel of Darkness, and walk in ways of darkness
(1QS3:15ff.).[13]

In both writings, the principles of light and darkness are evident.
Yet despite the similarity, the difference is obvious: in the Gospel according to John, the only-begotten Son of God has come into the world
to overcome darkness and to proclaim the victory. For the Qumran
community, however, a tremendous conflict is raging between the
Prince of Light and the Angel of Darkness; only the members of the
community are "children of light" (1QS 1:9) and the rest of humanity
are the children of darkness who must be hated by the children of light.
Hence, the members of the Qumran community had to withdraw
themselves from the world in complete separation. They had to "do the
truth" — in both the Qumran scrolls and in John's writings *truth* is one
of the key words — while John records Jesus' word addressed to the
unbelieving Jews: "If you continue in my word, you are truly my disciples; and you will know the truth, and the truth will make you free"
(John 8:31f.).

Of course, the themes of light and darkness, truth and perversity, are
not limited to the writings of John; they occur in the Pauline Epistles,
too. Paul reminds the Thessalonians that they are "children of the light
and children of the day. We are not of the night nor of darkness"
(I Thess. 5:5). However, this similarity has nothing to do with de-
pendence as if Paul had been in contact with the community at Qumran. The similarity of expressions comes forth out of a world of thought
which was common to the religious community near the Dead Sea and
the early Christian Church.

The Epistle to the Hebrews does not show any direct similarity in
wording. Yet in the method employed of quoting Scripture and commenting on the quoted passage, the resemblance of the so-called pesher
(commentary) on Biblical books such as Habakkuk and Nahum is
striking. Throughout his epistle, the author of Hebrews quotes passages
from the Psalms, from the Pentateuch, and from the Prophets; and
apart from citing the familiar text "the just shall live by faith" (Heb.
2:4), the writer seems to have nothing in common except for the manner of commenting on a quoted text. Here the writers of the scrolls and
the author of Hebrews give indication of having been trained in the
same methodology.[14]

What then is the value of the Dead Sea Scrolls for the New Testa-

---

[13]T. H. Gaster, *The Scriptures of the Dead Sea Sect.* London: Secker & Warburg,
1957; p. 53.
[14]S. Kistemaker, *The Psalm Citations in the Epistle to the Hebrews,* Amsterdam:
Van Soest, 1961.

ment? In brief, it is Professor Menahem Mansoor who gives the answer
to this question. Says he, "The paramount importance of the scrolls to
New Testament studies is that they add to our knowledge and understanding of the immediate pre-Christian era and give us a more precise
insight into the life and faith of one of the sects of the time."[15]

III. PAPYRI

New Discoveries

"If so many discoveries have been made in our own generation, there
is every reason to hope that more discoveries may still be awaiting us in
the sands of Egypt." Frederick G. Kenyon penned these prophetic
words in the last paragraph of his *The Text of the Greek Bible* in 1936.
Kenyon wrote when enthusiasms ran high; five years earlier, Sir Chester
Beatty had purchased a set of papyrus leaves which contained most of
the New Testament and which ranged in date from about A.D. 200 to
300. To be precise, Beatty had purchased a text of the New Testament
which, at that time, was well within two hundred years of the original
manuscripts. In fact, some of the leaves dated from about the year 200.
Kenyon edited the papyrus leaves which were subsequently published
by the British Museum and placed in the Beatty Museum located in a
suburb of Dublin. About thirty leaves, belonging to the same collection,
were bought by the University of Michigan from a dealer in Cairo,
Egypt.

Kenyon had before him a third century text of the New Testament,
which soon became known as the Beatty Papyri and received the num-
bers P^{45}, P^{46}, and P^{47} in the papyri series. P^{45} consisted of thirty leaves
which are the remnant of a codex of the four Gospels and Acts; that is,
there are two leaves for Matthew, six for Mark, seven for Luke, two for
John, and thirteen for Acts.

The next eighty-six leaves, designated P^{46}, belong to a codex which
lists the Pauline Epistles and Hebrews in the following order: Romans,
Hebrews, I and II Corinthians, Ephesians, Galatians, Philippians, Colossians, I and II Thessalonians. All the leaves are somewhat mutilated
and large segments of Romans and I Thessalonians, as well a II Thessalonians in its entirety, are missing.

And the last ten pages, also somewhat mutilated, bearing the number
P^{47}, belonged to a codex of the Revelation of John. The original codex
must have been more than three times the number of pages now comprising P^{47}. The first and the last part of the original codex are no

---

[15]*Op. cit.*, p. 162.

longer extant, but the ten pages which Beatty collected have the text of Revelation 9:10 through 17:2.

To add to the joy of discoveries, the oldest papyrus fragment of the New Testament was found rather accidentally in 1934. This fragment, known as P^{52}, contains two verses of John 18 and dates from about A.D. 125. Though the fragment had been purchased in Egypt as early as 1920, it remained hidden for fourteen years until C. H. Roberts happened to study unpublished papyri of the John Rylands Library in Manchester, England.

With all these exciting discoveries fresh in his memory, Kenyon looked toward the future and wished for more papyrus leaves from the sands of Egypt. However, more than twenty years had to elapse before the news of papyri discoveries once more elated New Testament scholars. This time the happy tidings came from Switzerland. Martin Bodmer had purchased a papyrus codex of the Fourth Gospel which dates from about A.D. 200; and in 1956, Victor Martin, Professor at the University of Geneva, published it. The papyrus codex is known as P^{66}, contains most of the first fourteen chapters of John, and totals some 104 pages. Besides, a number of fragments of this same codex were published two years later. These fragments contain much of the text of the remaining chapters of John's Gospel.

This codex was not the only one acquired by Martin Bodmer. His library in Geneva soon possessed a codex of the Epistle of Jude and the First and Second Epistles of Peter; it was presumably written early in the third century. Besides the three canonical epistles, the codex provides the text of Psalm 33 and Psalm 34 and some apocryphal books. In the catalog of papyrus documents, this codex is known as P^{72}.

Whereas P^{72} was published in 1959, two years later the so-called Bodmer Papyrus XVII, known as P^{74}, appeared in print. Also, this papyrus codex is housed in Martin Bodmer's Genevan library. It dates from the seventh century and contains portions of Acts and portions of the General Epistle of James, First and Second Peter, First, Second, and Third John, and Jude.

And the last papyrus codex from the Bodmer library is P^{75}, which dates from the end of the second to the first two decades of the third century. It contains the Gospels of Luke and John, of which the greater part has been preserved; that is, of the original 144 pages in the codex, a total of 102 have withstood the centuries. This codex is most valuable in respect to its age; it provides the earliest text thus far of the Gospel of Luke and it supplements, if not surpasses, P^{66} in furnishing one of earliest texts of the Fourth Gospel.[16]

---

[16]Cf. B. M. Metzger, *The Text of the New Testament*. New York & London: Oxford, 1964; pp. 36-42.

The Beatty Papyri and the collection of Bodmer have added greatly toward establishing a more accurate text of the New Testament. Despite the fact that the total number of manuscripts which have either all or part of the New Testament is approximately five thousand, the number of manuscripts from the second and third centuries are remarkably few. "For the Apocalypse, only four early witnesses survive from the third, fourth, and fifth centuries, P⁴⁷, ℵ (Sinaiticus), A (Alexandrinus), C (Ephraem Syrus). Therefore, the problem of establishing the critical texts of the earliest recensions of any local types, to say nothing of the original text, must in each case rest upon a few witnesses for any portion of the New Testament."[17] In other words, the vast number of Greek manuscripts belongs to a later date, running from A.D. 600 to A.D. 1000. This is not to say that all these manuscripts are without value, but that they are centuries removed from the original documents.

New Light on the New Testament Text

Though new papyri discoveries are very welcome, it is a fact that many years of painstaking research go by before the textual evidence of recently acquired manuscripts has been assimilated. After Beatty and the Bodmer papyri were edited, scholars needed sufficient time to analyze the texts and to relate their research to a common archetype. They realized that despite the second and third century dates of the manuscripts, a gap of about one hundred and fifty years still existed between manuscript and original document.

Nevertheless, this gap can be bridged to a great extent when the work of skillful editors in the Egyptian city of Alexandria is considered. The oldest papyri come from Egypt and, it is assumed, go back to the work Alexandrian correctors performed during the first and second centuries in Alexandria. Here writing was subjected to high standards of accuracy, correctors gathered manuscripts about A.D. 100 and published a standard text of the New Testament. Gunther Zuntz puts it in these words: "The Alexandrian work on the text of the Scriptures was a long process rather than a single act. Its beginnings were inconspicuous, and roughly 150 years passed before it culminated in the 'Euthalian' edition. Prior to this final achievement, the Alexandrian correctors strove, in ever repeated efforts, to keep the text current in their sphere free from the many faults that had infected it in the previous period and which tended to crop up again even after they had been obelized. These labours . . . resulted in the emergence of a type of text (as distinct from a definite edition) which served as a norm for the correctors

---

[17]K. W. Clark, "The Manuscripts of the Greek New Testament" *New Testament Manuscript Studies.* Chicago: University of Chicago Press, 1950; p. 4.

in provincial Egyptian scriptoria. The final result was the survival of a text far superior to that of the second century, even though the revisers, being fallible humans, rejected some of its correct readings and introduced some faults of their own."[18]

Throughout the second century, a segment of the church must have demonstrated a healthy respect for the exact wording of the standard text. And the link between this text and that of the recently discovered papyrus codices can be established with certainty.

Conclusion

Besides the valuable discoveries of Biblical manuscripts, a multitude of Greek papyri has been discovered in the sands of Egypt, consisting of private letters, government reports, military records, wills and testimonies, business accounts, and all kinds of interesting notes pertaining to the every-day life of people living in the Near East. All these papyri manuscripts proved that many of the words found in the New Testament and which had been considered "Biblical Greek" were an integral part of the common Greek spoken in the first century A.D. Moreover, they proved that the Greek in which the New Testament is written (Koine Greek = common Greek) was the language in use throughout the Roman Empire during the first centuries of the Christian era. These papyri have shown that Koine Greek, because it was spoken nearly everywhere in the Roman Empire, was in those days a world language — much the same as English is today. And last but not least, these manuscripts have contributed immensely · to a better understanding of the vocabulary, the syntax, the idioms, and the style of the language in which the New Testament has been written.

---

[18]*The Text of the Epistles.* London: British Academy, 1953; pp. 271f.

2. READINGS

I. TRANSLATIONS

From the beginning of the twentieth century, at least fifty translations of the Bible in the English language have appeared in print.[1] The more common are the Revised Standard Version, the Berkeley Version, the Confraternity Version, Phillips' Translation, Today's English Version (*Good News Bible*), the Jerusalem Bible, the New English Bible, The New International Version, and the New American Standard Bible. Certainly, translators have acted in response to a resolution adopted by the First International Conference of Bible Translators held at Zeist, the Netherlands, in 1947. The delegates to this conference determined that every fifty years a new translation should appear in print in any given language. In the light of the many translations, the translators have more than adhered to the resolution adopted in 1947. A fifty-year span allows for a new translation every second generation; that is, while the old generation still lives by the old translation, the next generation gets accustomed to a new version.

Anyone who has memorized portions of the time-honored King James Version and venerates the text of this translation will have some difficulty reading and accepting the modern versions. For example, in current translations he does not find the doxology to the Lord's Prayer in Matthew 6:13. The prayer ends with the sixth petition, "And lead us not into temptation, but deliver us from evil." In the Revised Standard Version, he discovers that the Gospel according to Mark ends at 16:8 with these words: "And they went out and fled from the tomb; for trembling and astonishment had come upon them; and they said nothing to any one, for they were afraid." The last twelve verses of Mark's Gospel have been put in small print in a footnote, without any word of

---

[1]Dewey M. Beegle, *God's Word Into English*. Grand Rapids: Eerdmans, 1960; pp. 121f.

explanation for deleting them from the text. He also notes that John 5:4 has been omitted, and that John 7 ends with verse 52 instead of 53, and that the whole passage concerning the woman caught in adultery (the first eleven verses of John 8), without any stated reason, has been relegated to a footnote in small print. And he sees that the familiar passage of the King James Version, often used to prove the doctrine of the trinity, I John 5:7, "For there are three that bear record in heaven, the Father, the Word, and the Holy Ghost: and these three are one," is not found in any of the modern translations.

Because no explanation is given for the omission of individual verses and substantial passages, the uninformed reader of the New Testament feels that part of Scripture has been left out. The explanation that other texts and versions add Mark 16:9-20 though omitted here, does not clarify the matter for him. Nor does the prefatory remark to the footnote at John 7:52 answer every question: "Other ancient authorities add 7:53—8:11 either here or at the end of this gospel or after Luke 21:38, with variations of the text."[2] Some of the recent translations leave the disputed passages in the text but enclose them within parentheses. One even gives an explanatory note at the end of the Gospel of Mark, "The ending with 'for' in the eighth verse, which is that way in the Greek, suggests an abrupt breaking off as if a leaf in Mark's writings had been mislaid. What follows is strictly in agreement with the other Gospels but contains nothing we could not otherwise possess."[3] At times, another shorter ending is added to the Second Gospel. Understandably, the reader of the New Testament is asking for an explanation.

II. TEXTUAL CRITICISM

We simply do not have a standard text for the New Testament. Instead we have a multitude of manuscripts which contain part or all of the New Testament. We have approximately 5,000 manuscripts in Greek, 8,000 in Latin, and some 1,000 in a number of other languages. And no manuscript is identical to another.

The Mohammedans do not have this problem in regard to their holy book, the Koran. "When the Caliph Othmann fixed a text of the Koran and destroyed all the old copies which differed from his standard, he provided for the uniformity of subsequent manuscripts at the cost of their historical foundation."[4] In other words, the Koran no longer rests upon a trustworthy basis; it rests upon the judgment of Caliph Oth-

    [2]*Revised Standard Version*. Cleveland and New York: World Publishing Company, 1962.
    [3]*Berkeley Version*. Grand Rapids: Zondervan, 1965.
    [4]B. F. Westcott, *Some Lessons of the Revised Version of the New Testament*, 4th ed. London, 1903; p. 8.

mann and the text which he fixed. This cannot be said of the New Testament: all the thousands of manuscripts which still exist are eloquent testimony that Christianity's historical foundation is truthworthy.

Original Manuscripts

Why do we have so many manuscripts? This question is almost the same as: "Why are there so many people of a given nationality? The answer to the last question is, rather simply: The parents bring forth children, who in turn have children. Though parents and children may look alike, they nevertheless differ individually. Likewise, the parent manuscripts, referred to as *autographa,* brought forth copies which in turn were copied. And because the manuscripts were copied by hand, variation in the text was inevitable. Just as people are part of a family, so manuscripts are taken up in families. And as people taken up in families resemble a tree with trunk, branches, and twigs, so manuscripts can be traced with the aid of a "family tree." In short, by tracing the family tree the New Testament scholar is able to come to a text similar to that of the original documents, the *autographa.*

Because the original manuscripts have been lost, the textual critic must work with the descendants of the parent document. In the descendants he finds not only surpassing agreement in the reading of the text, but also many variants. By examining the variants in the light of external (other manuscripts) and internal evidence, he is able to determine the reading similar to the original.

Variants

What caused the appearance of variants? This is an interesting question; it will take a little time to answer the question fully because it brings us back to the era of the scribe.

Many of the variants resulted from unintentional changes on the part of the scribe. In the early manuscripts, words were not separated and punctuation marks were not in use, so that misunderstanding of the exact reading was commonplace. As can be seen from the following example, THEBOOKISNOWHERE, misunderstanding cannot be avoided. Does the sentence read THE BOOK IS NOW HERE or THE BOOK IS NOWHERE? Moreover, when letters are placed close to each other without any breaks, the possibility of confusing one letter for another is great. A case in point is I Timothy 3:16, where some manuscripts read "God was manifested" and others "who was manifested."

Other errors arose from mistakenly copying a word or a letter twice, or writing it once when it should have been copied twice. Most of the time, external and internal evidence shows that the scribe made an error. However, there are cases in which it is very difficult to determine whether a word or letter belongs in the text or should be deleted. Thus, in Acts 27:37 most manuscripts read: "We were in all two hundred and seventy-six," yet others have this reading "We were in all about seventy-six." The copying of a letter twice accounts for the difference.

Still other errors are the result of faulty hearing, poor memory, and mistaken judgment. Just as in English such words as "here" and "hear" are pronounced the same, so in Greek many words, vowels, and diphthongs sounded alike. Does the text in Romans 5:1 read: "let us have peace with God" or "we have peace with God"? And because the Epistles to the Ephesians and to the Colossians are in places parallel and similar in content, scribes have occasionally copied words and phrases which properly belonged to the other epistle.

But mistakes were also made intentionally; introduced, no doubt, in an attempt to improve the text. In the manuscript used by the scribe, a sentence may not have been phrased correctly; thus, in the interest of the readers, the scribe changed the text by removing the error of grammar or logic. A well-meaning scribe changed the text of Revelation 1:5 from "loosed us from our sins" to "washed us from our sins."

Doctrinal Changes

And, at times, scribes introduced intentional doctrinal changes, invariably to emphasize the orthodox teaching of the church. A good example of this is the trinitarian passage of I John 5:7f. (as recorded in the KJV). The text which has the words Father, Word, and Holy Ghost is found in the Latin Vulgate which dates from the fourth century. However, when Erasmus in 1516 prepared an edition of the Greek New Testament, he did not find the trinitarian passage in any of the Greek manuscripts available to him. Consequently, he did not incorporate the passage in his first edition of the Greek New Testament. When Erasmus was accused of having omitted this particular verse, he promised to include it in a subsequent edition of the New Testament, provided that someone could show him a Greek manuscript which contained the passage. When a Franciscan monk produced the manuscript with the passage, which by all appearance was composed from the Latin Vulgate, Erasmus fulfilled his promise and inserted the trinitarian passage in his third edition of the Greek New Testament. Only three other Greek manuscripts dating from the twelfth, fifteenth, and sixteenth century have the disputed passage. Though the translators of the King James Version followed the Latin Vulgate by including the spurious passage, all subsequent translations of the Bible have omitted the reading: "in heaven, the Father, the Word, and the Holy Ghost;

and these three are one. And there are three that bear witness in earth."

The Lord's Prayer

To say that the Lord's Prayer was used in the worship services of the early church is rather trite; but to say that the early church because of liturgical style may have added the well-known doxology "for thine is the kingdom, and the power, and the glory, forever, Amen" is new. Jesus taught the disciples to pray the six petitions of the Lord's Prayer, but the doxology — according to the manuscript evidence — is not original. The words of the doxology have a great affinity to the prayer of David recorded in I Chronicles 29, especially the verses 10 through 13.

The familiarity of the Lord's Prayer with the doxology, as used in the worship services, may have induced a scribe to insert the conclusion in the text of the Greek manuscript. The translators of the King James Version, relying on such a manuscript, have given the English-speaking world the doxology to the Lord's Prayer. Yet all later translations end the prayer with the sixth petition, "and lead us not into temptation, but deliver us from evil."

Ending of Mark's Gospel

What about the ending of Mark's Gospel? To insert a single phrase or verse is understandable, but when the passage extends over twelve verses the matter is different. This ending contains the resurrection account of Jesus and the parallel version of the Great Commission. To delete these twelve verses almost seems to border an open attack on the Gospel according to Mark. Yet, a cursory reading of Mark 16 already points up a difference in style and vocabulary between the first eight verses and the last twelve (as well as the fifteen chapters preceding them). The ending differs so much from the preceding that a break between verses 8 and 9 is most obvious: the women are the subject of verse 8, Jesus of verse 9; Mary Magdalene is mentioned in verse 1 and introduced again in verse 9; verse 1 is a description of time, "when the sabbath was past," and verse 9 reiterates this as, "early on the first day of the week." On the basis of internal evidence we can safely say that Mark did not write the last twelve verses of Chapter 16. However, it remains an open question who the author is, despite the information provided in a tenth century Armenian manuscript of the Gospel, which seems to indicate that the Presbyter Ariston (presumably a disciple of the Apostle John) wrote them.

Do these last twelve verses have strong manuscript support? The answer to this question must be negative. Though many manuscripts have the familiar ending, the better documents conclude the Gospel at Chapter 16:8. Also, a few late manuscripts do have a shorter ending to

Mark's Gospel in the following words: "But they reported to Peter and those with him all that they had been told. And after this Jesus himself sent out by means of them, from east to west, the sacred and imperishable proclamation of eternal salvation." However, support for the authenticity of this reading is next to nothing. Hence, the choice must be between adding the twelve verses or deleting them. As we have already seen, the textual evidence is for deletion.

Yet the question remains: Did Mark end his Gospel at verse 8? Indications are that he did not end on a note of fear ("for they were afraid"). The clause itself points to something more to follow; even though the verb can stand alone, the clause as such is incomplete. Moreover, the fact that others have written endings for Mark's Gospel is indicative of the incomplete ending. Perhaps Mark did write a conclusion which may have perished soon after. We can only guess; no more.

Ned B. Stonehouse is of the opinion that the abrupt ending of the Gospel is very well possible; the expression "to fear" should then be understood as reverential fear and not as cowering fear. On the basis of an exegetical study he asserts: "That reverential fear is in view in Mark 16:8, however, seems to be demanded by its association with amazement, astonishment and trembling, which, as the survey of Marcan usage indicates, characteristically point to an attitude of deferential awe."[5] And in respect to the personal manifestations of the resurrected Jesus, Mark does make clear that a personal appearance of Jesus is about to happen when the disciples and Peter shall have gone to Galilee: "there you will see him" (16:7).

The longer ending, nevertheless, was regarded as part of Mark's Gospel by the middle of the second century. Because the ending was added as an appendix in the middle of the second century already, some writers defend its authenticity. Says Donald Guthrie: "While it cannot be regarded as part of Mark's Gospel, it nevertheless represents an authentic account of resurrection appearances."[6]

Adultery Passage

The passage concerning the woman caught in adultery actually falls in the same category. The style and vocabulary of John 7:53—8:11 differs from the rest of the Gospel. Evidence for the fact that the passage does not belong here comes from a number of minor manuscripts which place the verses at the end of the Gospel of John. Still other

---

[5]*The Witness of Matthew and Mark to Christ.* Grand Rapids: Eerdmans, 2nd edition, 1958; p. 107.
[6]*The Gospel and Acts, New Testament Introduction.* Chicago: Tyndale Press, 1965; p. 75.

manuscripts insert the passage in the Gospel according to Luke, in between Chapters 21 and 22. Again, the textual support for omitting these verses after John 7:52 is strong, and translators have either omitted the passage or placed it within brackets.

III. LITERARY CRITICISM

Though the gospel of Jesus Christ is one gospel, related by Matthew, Mark, Luke, and John, the obvious fact brought home to the reader is that these four writers differ much in relating the gospel. Of course, the reader has no difficulty understanding differences when the evangelists are reporting historical incidents: the writers bring out different perspectives in their account of the incident. But when the Gospel writers quote the very words of Jesus, the reader does expect verbatim accounts of the actual words spoken by Jesus.

However, the Gospels do not present the very words of Jesus in a stereotype form. There are a number of variations in such familiar passages as the Beatitudes and the Lord's Prayer recorded in Matthew and in Luke. The reader may conclude that Jesus taught the Beatitudes twice: He taught them to the crowds seated along the hillside (Matt. 5:1ff.), and he taught them to the disciples and a great crowd of people in a level place (Luke 6:17ff.). Likewise, he may conclude that the Lord's Prayer was taught in the context of the Sermon on the Mount (Matt. 6:9-15), and at another time in response to the disciple's request: "Lord, teach us to pray" (Luke 11:2-4).

The average reader of the New Testament is content with this explanation; for him, the historicity of the spoken words of Jesus is safeguarded by means of this method of interpretation. And much can be said in favor of this method. First, the evangelists describe the local settings in which the teaching of Jesus took place — the one, a Galilean hillside; the other, a level place. Second, in the typical fashion of his day, Jesus taught the disciples and the crowds orally. Jesus never wrote anything down; variation in his address set him off from the scribes of his day. "The crowds were astonished at his teaching, for he taught them as one who has authority, and not as their scribes" (Matt. 7:28, 29). And third, Jesus did not speak his words once for all. As is evident from comparing parallel passages in the Gospels, he often repeated what he had said at other occasions; yet he did not repeat himself verbatim, but in response to the situation he altered his words to suit his purpose.

Parallel Accounts

When the New Testament scholar places parallel passages next to each other and studies the text in context, he asks the question whether the above-mentioned interpretation of the different wording of the sayings of Jesus is adequate. By viewing the accounts in parallel columns and by studying them in the context of the individual Gospel, he becomes aware of the method and purpose of the individual Gospel writer.

A look at the parallel columns of the Lord's Prayer is most helpful:

Matthew 6:9-13	*Luke 11:2-4*
Our Father who art in heaven,	Father,
Hallowed be thy name,	Hallowed be thy name.
Thy kingdom come,	Thy kingdom come.
Thy will be done,	
On earth as it is in heaven.	
Give us this day our daily bread;	Give us this day our daily bread;
And forgive us our debts,	And forgive us our sins,
As we also have forgiven our debtors;	For we ourselves forgive everyone who is indebted to us;
And lead us not into temptation,	And lead us not into temptation.
But deliver us from evil.	

It is true that the two renditions of the Lord's Prayer in the King James Version are nearly identical, except that in Luke the doxology is omitted. But because of the tremendous research which has been going on in establishing the purest text possible, in the last one hundred years every translation gives the longer version of the Lord's Prayer in Matthew, the shorter in Luke.

If these versions are seen against the background and purpose of the evangelists, many questions concerning the differences receive an answer. Matthew wrote his Gospel for Jewish-Christians; Luke addressed the Gospel to Greek-speaking Christians. Says Joachim Jeremias: "The differences in these two primers on prayer are to be explained by the fact that they are directed at very different groups of people. The Matthaean catechism on prayer is addressed to people who have learned to pray in childhood but whose prayer stands in danger of becoming a routine. The Lucan catechism on prayer, on the other hand, is addressed to people who must for the first time learn to pray and whose courage to pray must be roused. It is clear that Matthew is transmitting to us instruction on prayer directed at Jewish-Christians, Luke at Gentile-Christians."[7]

The Jewish Christians had taken along a rich liturgical tradition when they became Christians. For instance, the address of the Lord's Prayer is simply "Father" in Luke's version, but in that of Matthew the address is given in the form of a typical Jewish invocation: "Our Father who art in heaven." In this characteristically Jewish address, the

---

[7]*The Prayers of Jesus.* Naperville, Illinois: Allenson, 1967; pp. 88f.

petitioner approaches God in trustful relationship by calling him "Our Father." At the same time, he is mindful of the separation which exists between heaven and earth. That particular point is stressed in the third petition: "Thy will be done, on earth as it is in heaven." The Gentile-Christian merely uttered the word "Father" in addressing God.

Which of the two versions of the Lord's Prayer is the original? To say that Jesus taught the Prayer twice in exactly the form as we find it in Matthew and in Luke is an answer, though inadequate and incomplete. Could it be that Jesus taught the disciples (and the crowds) a general model of the Lord's Prayer which, in the course of time because of its liturgical use in the Jewish-Christian churches and in the Gentile-Christian churches, underwent some changes?

A few remarks are in order at this point. First, that the Lord's Prayer assumed a significant place in the liturgy of the early Christian church may never be taken lightly. "As one of the most holy treasures of the church, the Lord's Prayer, together with the Lord's Supper, was reserved for full members, and it was not disclosed to those who stood outside."[8] Second, just as today prayers are concluded in the name of Jesus, so in the early Christian church, in accordance with Jewish practice, prayers were ended by means of a statement of praise and honor to God the Father. This doxology was not part of the actual prayer itself and could be changed as the occasion demanded. In time, such a doxology was added to the written text of the Lord's Prayer in Matthew's Gospel and, through these later manuscripts, became inseparably connected with it. Even today, no Christian praying the Lord's Prayer would end with the last petition and omit the doxology: "For thine is the kingdom and the power and the glory, for ever. Amen." Yet the most reliable manuscripts do not have the doxology. Therefore, it is not considered Scriptural, even though Christians conclude the Lord's Prayer with this well-known doxology.

A third remark concerns the language in which Jesus taught the Lord's Prayer. Though Jesus did speak Greek occasionally, his mother tongue was Aramaic, as is evident from many expressions in the Gospels. Thus, Jesus taught the Lord's Prayer in his mother tongue and, perhaps during his ministry, it was already translated into Greek. The fifth petition is most revealing in this respect: Matthew speaks of debts, Luke of sins. In the second part of the fifth petition both Matthew and Luke refer to debtors. What did Jesus teach? Did he say: forgive us our debts, or forgive us our sins? The Aramaic language has a word for "sins" which has the meaning of "debts." In the Gospel of Matthew, this Aramaic word has been translated literally into Greek; the reading is "debts." But in Luke's Gospel the general Greek word for sins is used,

[8]*Ibid.,* p. 85.

which has no implication of debt. Yet in the second part of the petition, Luke has the reading: "for we ourselves forgive everyone who is indebted to us." This part not only points to the fact that the word "sins" in the first part has the meaning of "debts," but also that the underlying Aramaic is original.

We conclude, therefore, that Jesus taught the Lord's Prayer in his mother tongue. The question remains whether Jesus himself gave the church a longer and a shorter version of this prayer. We believe that Jesus uttered the prayer twice in two different versions. But it is also possible that both Matthew and Luke reflect the use of the Lord's Prayer in the setting of Aramaic speaking Christians with a rich liturgical background, and of Greek-speaking Christians who had come out of the Gentile world and were devoid of liturgy. When Matthew and Luke wrote their individual Gospel accounts, the Lord's Prayer had become a sacred treasure for some decades already, both in the Aramaic-speaking church and in the Greek-speaking church. Matthew, writing his Gospel for the Jews, would take the prayer in the form in which it was treasured by Jewish-Christians. Likewise, Luke would incorporate the Lord's Prayer in his Gospel in the form in which it was prayed by Gentile-Christians.

Purpose of the Evangelists

When we read the Gospels, we hear the living voice of Jesus speaking to us. The very words of Jesus are dear to every believing Christian. Even though we have the words of Jesus recorded in the four Gospels, we may not think of them in terms of present methods of recording words and voices in a daily newscast.

Differences in recording the words of Jesus become apparent in looking at parallel passages in Matthew and Luke. For example, Matthew constantly speaks about "the kingdom of heaven." Luke, however, records the words "kingdom of God." Why would Matthew have Jesus say "kingdom of heaven" and Luke, in the same setting and context, have him use the expression "kingdom of God"? Jesus could have spoken only one of the two expressions. Who reports the very words of Jesus faithfully?

The answer to this question lies in the purpose of the evangelist. Whereas the expression "kingdom of heaven" comes out of an Aramaic context, this same expression would not have been fully understood by Greek-speaking Christians with a Gentile background. Matthew wrote his Gospel for his Jewish readers living in Palestine. He undoubtedly put down the words which he heard Jesus speak. But Luke addressed his Gospel to the Hellenic world bordering the Mediterranean Sea. He knew that the expression "kingdom of heaven" would not convey the intended meaning; the words would be misunderstood in Asia Minor and Greece where people had a different conception of heaven than the Jews in Palestine. In order to keep the intended meaning, Luke had to substitute the word "God" for "heaven." By means of this substitution, the intent remained the same though the words differed.

In one of the longest parallel passages, recorded both in Matthew's Gospel and in Luke's, a similar change in wording occurs. Except for an extra sentence in Luke, the passages in Matthew 7:7-11 and Luke 11:9-13 are identical. The passages are introduced by the familiar text: "Ask, and it will be given you." The change, however, occurs in the concluding verse of this rather lengthy passage:

Matthew 7:11	Luke 11:13
If you then, who are evil, know how to give good gifts to your children, how much more will your Father who is in heaven give *good things* to those who ask him.	If you then, who are evil, know how to give good gifts to your children, how much more will the heavenly Father give the *Holy Spirit* to those who ask him.

The italicized words point out the difference. Did Jesus say "good things" or "the Holy Spirit"? We could say that Jesus taught these words twice in slightly differing forms, were it not for the fact that we have to take account of the purpose of the evangelists. When Matthew uses the expression "good things," his Jewish readers had no difficulty understanding him. They were schooled in the Old Testament Scriptures in which the expression referred to both spiritual and material blessings. For them, spiritual blessings were the good things of life, as is clear from the prophecy of Isaiah: "How beautiful upon the mountains are the feet of him who brings good tidings, who publishes peace, who brings good tidings of good, who publishes salvation." Isaiah proclaimed good news, which consisted of the spiritual blessing of salvation. Thus when the Jewish-Christians read the words "good things" in Matthew's Gospel, they would think of salvation and peace.

Luke, writing for the Greek-speaking world, could not use the expression "good things" without losing its significance. Certainly, Luke could have written the words as they are found in Matthew's Gospel, but his readers would not think of salvation and peace; they would understand the words to mean material prosperity. In fact, in the next chapter of his Gospel, Luke uses the word "goods." In the parable the rich fool says: "I will pull down my barns, and build larger ones, and there I will store all my grain and my *goods*. And I will say to my soul, Soul, you have ample *goods* laid up for many years" (12:18 f.). The Greek word simply did not convey the meaning found in the Aramaic-speaking world for this same word. The Gentile-

Christian thought of earthly possessions, not of spiritual blessings. In order to bring out the correct meaning, Luke had to substitute the expression. And by means of the substitution from "good things" to "the Holy Spirit," his readers would think of the blessings of salvation and peace.

Do we have the exact words and all the words of Jesus in the Gospels? Certainly we would like to answer that question in the affirmative because the Gospel belongs to Jesus Christ, as Mark puts it in the introduction to his account. But in view of the many changes in the wording of the sayings of Jesus and the incomplete collection of sayings of Jesus in the Gospels, the answer to the question must be in the negative. Let us take the last part of the question first. The saying of Jesus, "It is more blessed to give than to receive," is not found in any of the four Gospels, but in Acts 20:35. Why was this word of Jesus, well-known to the church of the first century, not recorded in the Gospels?

Second, if we ask for the exact words of Jesus because they are holy, we want the words of Jesus in the language which he spoke. But if language were holy, the words of Jesus should have been preserved in Aramaic, because that was the language he spoke. Apart from a few sayings, such as *talitha cumi, ephphatha,* and *Eloi, Eloi, lama sabachthani,* no Aramaic is found in the Gospels. The Holy Spirit chose the common, every-day Greek of that time to relate divine revelation. The sacredness of the words of Jesus is not inherent in the words as such, but in the message conveyed. Think of Pentecost in the city of Jerusalem, where the message of salvation came to the people in many languages. The common words of the people carried the sacred message of God's love in Jesus Christ. Therefore, inspired by the Holy Spirit, the evangelists wrote their Gospels in so-called *Koine* Greek, which was the Greek language in use by common people living in countries bordering the Mediterranean Sea during the first century. In that language the words of Jesus were recorded, fully inspired, yet used by the evangelists in such a way that the message of the words reached the people they addressed.

Interdependence

Because Luke was not an apostle but a follower of the Apostles Paul and Peter, he had to receive his information for the Third Gospel from "eyewitnesses and ministers of the Word," as he writes in the Introduction to the Gospel. But he also mentions that "many have undertaken to compile a narrative of things which have been accomplished among us" (1:1) and that on the basis of information gathered, he is going to write an orderly account of all that had transpired. Luke does not wish to imply that those who had written a Gospel had not done their work well and that he would set things straight in his account. He merely records a statement of fact: there are other Gospel accounts in circulation. These accounts could be the Gospels of Matthew and Mark; and Luke, not only relying on the testimony of the "eyewitnesses and ministers of the Word," may have consulted the written accounts of the other evangelists.

That Luke depended on oral tradition is clear from his statement concerning the eyewitnesses who delivered the narrative to him orally. And that he relied on written reports is evident from his statement that other Gospel accounts existed. The question is whether he borrowed reports from either Matthew or Mark or both. By comparing the Gospels of Matthew, Mark, and Luke, the New Testament scholar has learned some interesting facts. "First, Matthew and Luke follow Mark's order for the most part; second, in numerous specific points . . . Matthew and Luke, in pursuing their own particular aims, depart from Mark's order of events; and third, *Matthew and Luke never depart from Mark in the same way.*"[9]

This rather condensed summary of New Testament scholarship means this: for centuries the sequence Matthew-Mark-Luke was unquestioned and still is by some scholars; Matthew was written first, Mark depended upon the written Gospel of Matthew, and Luke depended upon both Matthew and Mark. Augustine in the fourth century already advocated this sequence, which, of course, is based on the order given them in the New Testament. A comparison of Matthew's Gospel and Mark's Gospel shows that, though the Second Gospel is shorter in the individual stories, Mark provides many more details than Matthew. Because of this observation, Mark's Gospel is given priority and is called the Gospel upon which the others depend. The most important argument in this observation is that Matthew and Luke never depart from Mark in the same way. That is, Matthew and Luke have much material in common which is in harmony with the order in the Gospel of Mark.

Could it be, scholars have asked, that Matthew and Luke have depended on a second source? If the Gospel of Mark is the first source of written information, was there another source which has been lost in the course of the first century? Some scholars say that this is indeed the case. Guided by the suggestion of the German theologian and philosopher Friedrich Schleiermacher, who in 1832 referred to such a source as Q, an abbreviation for the German word Quelle (source), they assert that the writers of the Gospels of Matthew and Luke relied

[9]G. E. Ladd, *The New Testament and Criticism.* Grand Rapids: Eerdmans, 1967; p. 126.

upon this source as well as the Gospel of Mark when they gathered their material for the composition of their accounts. "This material . . . embraces about 235 verses and contains chiefly sayings of Jesus, though some narrative material, including the miraculous healing of the centurion's servant, is present as well. . . . Though several scholars believe that this material circulated only in oral form, most hold that it was reduced to writing, perhaps in Aramaic and then in Greek, before it was utilized by Matthew and Luke."[10]

However, there is no unanimity among scholars about the source called Q because of its hypothetical nature. Some maintain that Q was a written document used by Matthew and Luke. But objections to this view are rather strong because no such document has ever been found among the papyri discoveries; also, if Matthew and Luke had relied on such a document, the texts which are parallel would not have differed much. This fact would seem to indicate that two documents called Q existed during the first century. Other scholars, though rejecting the existence of a written document, are willing to consider an oral source called Q. That would mean that both Matthew and Luke drew their common material from oral tradition. The many and varied hypotheses concerning this source led one New Testament scholar to write an article entitled, "Q is what you make it."[11] However, in view of the great similarity between the Gospel accounts of Matthew and Luke, it is unfair to rule out the possibility of reliance on a source which is no longer extant. The conclusion to which Donald Guthrie comes is considerate and valuable. Says he: "Luke's use of Matthew cannot be pronounced impossible, although it is not without special difficulties of its own. It is perhaps preferable to suppose that early catechetical instruction included much of the teaching of Jesus and this would be imparted according to a fixed pattern. Hence the Q material may well have existed in an oral form of a sufficiently fixed character to account for both the verbal similarities and differences. Alternatively it may be conjectured that part of the sayings material was reduced to writing in the form of brief notes and that these were used by Matthew and Luke and supplemented by other oral traditions. . . . In a field of study in which there is so much which must be considered conjectural, it would be foolish to be dogmatic."[12]

[10]B. M. Metzger, The New Testament, Its Background, Growth, and Content. New York, Nashville: Abingdon, 1965; p. 83.
[11]C. S. Petrie,Novum Testamentum 3 (1959); pp. 28-33.
[12]New Testament Introduction. The Gospels and Acts. Chicago: Intervarsity, 1965; pp. 149f.

3. CRITICISM

If there is one word which applies universally to the New Testament of late, it is the word *criticism*. We mention only one of the factors responsible for this rising tide of criticism: the discovery of ancient manuscripts. These manuscripts have greatly stimulated a critical study of the New Testament text. Though the work of bringing together, comparing, and checking the textual evidence of the various manuscripts is tedious and time-consuming, the New Testament scholar who takes on the task of textual criticism has been, and is being, amply rewarded for his labors. He knows that he has given the church a text much purer than it ever possessed before.

However, textual criticism is only a segment of the entire field of critical New Testament studies. For more than a century, the expression *source criticism* has been used; this criticism, as the term implies, is a study of the sources available to the evangelists when they composed the Gospels. When this study failed to satisfy the New Testament scholar, because of limited possibilities and great uncertainty, he turned his attention to form criticism. Form criticism became known due to the studies of Karl Ludwig Schmidt, Martin Dibelius, and Rudolf Bultmann, about 1920. These men studied the form in which the evangelists presented the individual Gospel narrative.

The results of form-critical studies have not always been positive and assuring; in fact, dissatisfaction with these results has kept some scholars completely outside the academic circle of form criticism, while others have attempted to move from form criticism to redaction criticism. Redaction criticism has been championed by such men as Günther Bornkamm, Willi Marxsen, and Hans Conzelmann, and concerns the composition of the individual Gospel. And if this area, which relatively speaking is still in the infancy stage, is not sufficient to today's scholar, he may turn his attention to another area of criticism in New Testament studies. J. Arthur Baird has introduced the term audience criticism. This is a study in which the hypothesis is advanced that Jesus in his teaching adapted his words selectively to his audience.

These are the areas in which the student of the New Testament has been and is engaged. Naturally, the question must be raised: What has been achieved in these areas of criticism?

I. SOURCE CRITICISM

Early Sources

The discoveries in the sands of Egypt and around the Dead Sea have confirmed one fact: collections of sayings of Jesus and collections of Old Testament Scripture passages were in circulation during the first century of the Christian era. The Gospel of Thomas with its 114 sayings of Jesus is a case in point: sayings of Jesus were collected in written form apart from the canonical Gospels. Moreover, the Dead Sea manuscripts confirmed the assumption that the practice of collecting sayings or Scripture passages relating to the Messiah was customary among the Jewish people.

A study of the Gospels necessarily includes and concerns the sources which the writers of the Gospels employed. Comments British theologian Vincent Taylor: "But while the Gospels themselves are comparatively late, they rest upon earlier sources, some of which were written. Only so can we explain the astonishing verbal agreement between Matthew, Mark, and Luke, in many parallel passages, and the less striking but even more significant agreement often present in the order in which events and sayings are recorded."[1]

That written sources are the substratum of the Gospel of Luke is evident from his introductory sentence to the Third Gospel. He refers to those people who have composed a narrative concerning the things which took place during the life of Jesus. But how did Matthew and Mark write their Gospels? This question brings us right into the so-called Synoptic Problem. The first three Gospels are known as the Synoptics, a word derived from the Greek, which means, freely translated, "with one glance of the eye." That is, when the accounts of the first three Gospels are placed in parallel columns, the reader "with one glance of the eye" is able to see the basic similarity of the parallel texts. If the three Gospels were identical to one another, there would not be any need for three Gospels. But Matthew, Mark, and Luke are not identical. To mention one example: Matthew and Luke have birth narratives, Mark begins with the baptism of Jesus; and

---

[1]*The Gospels.* London: Epworth Press, 11th edition, 1967; p. 2.

the birth narratives of Matthew and Luke show no similarity at all. What were the sources used by the individual evangelist? That is the question known as the Synoptic problem.

Synoptic Problem

Already in the eighteenth century, the hypothesis was advanced that one of the written sources for Luke may have been the Gospel of Mark. In the years that followed, this "Marcan hypothesis" has been refined and supported by numerous arguments. The priority of Mark, for the great majority of scholars, has become the accepted theory. This theory concludes that the Gospels of Matthew and Luke have the Gospel of Mark as their primary source; the secondary source for these two Gospels consists of a collection of sayings of Jesus, commonly designated as Q (for the German word *Quelle*). Besides these two sources, both Matthew and Luke may have used material peculiar to each. The source of Matthew is at times referred to as *M,* and the one for Luke as *L.*

Some scholars have objected to the priority of the Gospel of Mark, despite the contention that "Mark and Matthew sometimes agree in order against Luke, and Mark and Luke still more frequently against Matthew, while Matthew and Luke never agree in order against Mark."[2] Already in 1783, the German New Testament theologian Johann Jakob Griesbach submitted the hypothesis that Mark was written later than the Gospel of Luke and that the Second Gospel was dependent on Matthew and Luke. Since that time the priority of Mark has been challenged; in the last few decades especially Roman Catholic theologians have championed the priority of Matthew's Gospel.

John Chapman expressed his view on the priority of the First Gospel in a book which was posthumously published in 1937.[3] He was of the opinion that Peter, at Rome, used the Gospel of Matthew as textbook for preaching. Peter used the Aramaic text of Matthew's Gospel, and in his preaching brought out his own vivid recollections. Mark acted as Peter's secretary and wrote the Second Gospel. According to Chapman, the Greek Gospel of Matthew was written soon afterwards, so that, consequently, Luke was able to make use of the Gospels of Matthew and Mark. The conclusion of Chapman's argument is that the need for the hypothetical source Q has been eliminated entirely.

Basil C. Butler supported the same view in a book published in 1951. He placed the three Synoptic Gospels in the customary order

---

[2]F. F. Bruce, *The New Testament Documents. Are They Reliable?* 5th edition reprint, Grand Rapids: Eerdmans, 1967; p. 34.
[3]*Matthew, Mark, and Luke.* London, 1937.

of Matthew, Mark, and Luke and dismissed the whole Q hypothesis.[4]

Also in Protestant circles, the argument against Marcan priority
has been debated. In a scholarly presentation of the Synoptic problem,
William R. Farmer has presented his own approach. He does not
follow the order suggested by Roman Catholic theologians; instead,
he submits this argument: "Matthew appears to be the earliest Gospel,
and Luke seems next in order. . . . Luke seems to be dependent on
Matthew for the general order and form of his Gospel, and in many
instances he clearly copied his text from Matthew. There seems to be
no sound literary or historical ground on which to base a denial of
the premise that Mark is throughout the whole extent of his Gospel
working closely with texts of Matthew and Luke before him."[5]

A few decades ago, the question of the Synoptic problem seemed to
have been answered satisfactorily because the priority of Mark and
the existence of Q were established facts. Consequently, the study of
source criticism at that time came to an apparent standstill. This is
no longer the case. Scholars who have challenged the priority of Mark
have reopened the whole question. Certainly, only a few people question the Marcan hypothesis; the majority of scholars have accepted
it as fact. Nevertheless, there is general agreement that the question
concerning the order of Gospel formation has taken source criticism
off the dusty shelf and placed it on the lectern of debate.

II. FORM CRITICISM

For more than half a century, the word *form criticism* has been in
circulation. And, for that matter, the whole movement which this
word represents is hardly a modern theological trend. Yet the effect
of form criticism has been noticed only in the last few decades. Therefore, the study conducted by the form critics is not quite obsolete.

What is form criticism? Well, the name itself says quite a bit
already: a criticism of forms — forms, let us say, in the Gospels. The
individual Gospel stories are analyzed and criticized; the person doing
this type of work is called a form critic.

But let us go back to the very beginning. That is, we have to go
to Germany in 1901. There an Old Testament theologian wrote a
commentary on the book of Genesis. Theologian Hermann Gunkel
explained that many chapters of Genesis were individual stories which
had originated not as accounts of true historical events; they had
originated in the popular custom of people sitting around a camp

---

[4]*The Originality of Matthew.* Cambridge: University Press, 1951.
[5]*The Synoptic Problem.* New York: Macmillan; London: Collier-Macmillan, 1964;
pp. 200f.

fire in the evening or city officials sitting in the gateway of the city during the day. There, stories were told repeatedly for instruction and entertainment in the form of legends. They were told in succession and gradually assumed the form of a continuous narrative. However, the individual story within this succession was a separate unit. The core of this unit consisted of a proverb or a word of wisdom. In other words, a popular proverb happened to be much in vogue among the people, such as "love conquers everything." This proverb was applied to a given situation in life. Details were added, and gradually a fully developed story was told at the camp fire or in the city gate. Stories of this nature were linked together to form the narrative which eventually was recorded as chapters in the book of Genesis.

Nearly two decades later, New Testament theologians began to apply this method of criticizing the Biblical narrative to the Gospels. They had often looked at the short narratives of the Gospels and wondered how these individual units were ever put together to form the continuous story known as the gospel. They assumed that the separate units of the gospel at one time circulated orally in the early church. This assumption was further expanded: the stories were used in the worship services by the early church, in catechetical instruction, and in defense of the faith.

Honest Questions

Precisely now, what did the apostles do with the knowledge they had received from Jesus? What did they do with the knowledge of the words and the deeds of Jesus? If we may speak in approximate figures for just a moment, we say that Jesus ascended to heaven in the year 30, and that the first Gospel appearing in written form began to circulate in the year 60. Then the question arises: What happened to the knowledge of the words and deeds of Jesus during this thirty-year time span? Still another question may be asked: When the written Gospels did appear, why did the writers only include certain sayings of Jesus at the exclusion of others? The well-known saying, "It is more blessed to give than to receive," is not found in any of the four Gospels. Instead, it is found in the farewell speech of Paul, delivered on the beach of Miletus to the elders of the church at Ephesus. Why was this saying not taken up in the context of any or all of the four Gospels?

It is clear from the Gospels that only a select number of incidents from the life of Jesus have been recorded. If we assert, on the basis of the Fourth Gospel, that Jesus ministered to the people for a total of three years, then it is hard to believe that he raised only three people from the dead: the daughter of Jairus, the young man of Nain, and Lazarus. And it is difficult to accept that of the many sick whom Jesus healed, there are but few whose sight was restored (among them, Bartimaeus). No wonder that John ends the Fourth Gospel by saying: "But there are also many other things which Jesus did; were every one of them to be written, I suppose that the world itself could not contain the books that would be written" (21:25).

For more than half a century already, scholars have seriously studied the how, the where, and the when of Gospel-writing. Certainly, there was a time when New Testament scholars were satisfied to know that Matthew, publican and apostle, wrote the first Gospel; that Mark composed the Second Gospel guided by Peter; and that Luke received his information from "eyewitnesses and ministers of the Word." That time is now past. Students of the New Testament want to know how the Gospels were written during the second half of the first century.

Attempts

What New Testament theologians have done is to explore, in so far as this is possible, the unknown area of oral tradition. The so-called form critical theologian turned to a study of folklore. That is, some studied the structure of old-Norwegian oral tradition in which legends were presented and preserved. The results of such studies were applied to the four Gospels. The form critics reasoned that if a given pattern of folklore and tradition can be observed in one field, the same should hold for another field. If something holds true for the structure and formation of Norwegian folklore, the same should hold for the structure and formation of the New Testament Gospels.

Form critical theologians attempted to explain the fragmentary structure of the Gospels by setting forth a grand assumption. They assumed that the individual stories of the Gospel circulated orally within the early church. Moreover, they assumed that the Gospel units circulated individually in the form of separate, circumstantial reports. And they assumed that each report had been subjected to the rule of the early church; that is, they assumed that the early church accepted only those stories which filled the need created by the worship services, by catechetical instruction, and by the defense of the faith. In short, the collection of stories, now known as gospel, was a handbook for the church at worship, in the catechism room, and in the hall of public debate.

The task which the form critics have set for themselves is this: to reconstruct the development of the form in which the gospel was proclaimed orally. They trace the development of the oral gospel until the gospel was written down permanently. Actually, their task is to survey, historically, the formation of the Gospels. What form critics are doing is to study the history of the formation of the gospel. And this is exactly what the German name *Formgeschichte* means — form history.

What happened during those years of A.D. 30 to 60? The form critic answers this question by saying that there were numerous individual stories in circulation. These stories were eventually brought together much the same as a child strings beads for a necklace; they have no connecting links and have been collected and arranged at random by the gospel writer. For the sake of literary style, the writer may have put a few connecting links between the passages, but in reality we have — so to speak — individual beads.

Representatives

As early as 1919, German theologian Karl Ludwig Schmidt said that the individual units of the gospel were linked together, but that the links themselves did not form part of the stories. Links, in the opinion of Schmidt, were the references to places where the events happened, and to time and sequence when these things took place. These links merely served the purpose of making the gospel stories more attractive. But, said Schmidt, these details, though interesting, are void of any value.[6]

In that same year, 1919, another German scholar, Martin Dibelius, followed the approach of Schmidt. He studied the Gospels, worked out a method, and categorized the individual gospel stories. According to Dibelius, the various categories consisted of narrative tales, legends, the passion story, and myths.

Dibelius classified the healing of the blind man at Jericho (Mark 10:46-52) as a narrative tale. What does Dibelius do with this narrative? The core of the narrative consists of the faith of the man and the passion of Jesus; the rest of the story, such as the name Bartimaeus, the location of Jericho, the passing crowd, the hush to be silent, is descriptive detail made up by the evangelist.

An example of a legend can be found in Luke 2:41-52, which is the account of the twelve-year old Jesus in the temple. Asserts Dibelius, the core of the legend is located in the question: "How is it that you sought me? Did you not know that I must be in my Father's house?" All the other elements of the story — the worry and lack of understanding, the time reference of three days, and the return to Nazareth — have been added to the legend.

---

[6]*Der Rahmen der Geschichte Jesu.* Berlin: Trowitzsch, 1919.

Dibelius speaks of the legend of the empty tomb which has taken the place of the mythological account of the resurrection.[7] The baptism of Jesus, his temptation, and his transfiguration are mythological stories.

Rudolf Bultmann, emeritus professor of New Testament theology at the University of Marburg, Germany, has pushed the form critical approach to radical extremes. He boldly maintains that the majority of Jesus' words and works, as they are recorded in the four Gospels, must be considered a production of the early church. Certainly, says Bultmann, there are authentic sayings of Jesus; but whenever a saying of Jesus has been placed within the framework of a narrative in the Gospel unit, the narrative together with the saying must be regarded as the product of the early Christian community. Whenever Bultmann thinks that a certain Gospel unit could have been composed by the early church, he regards that unit as the product of the Christian community. The result is that the gospel, as understood by Bultmann, finds its birth and development in the early church.[8]

Why did the early Christian community construct these individual Gospel units? In the opinion of the form critic, the individual Gospel units were used by the church to proclaim the Word because these units were their expression of faith. Thus, the faith of the early Christians came to expression in these individual units. These units, in turn, were used to awaken faith in those people who listened to the preaching of the Word.

In the language of the form critic, the Gospel units were the *kerygma* of the church. The word *kerygma* has been taken from the Greek language and means proclamation. It is the message of salvation which the herald of the Word brings — the message of the early Christian church. This term, kerygma, is used by the form critic whenever he refers to the preaching of the early church.

If we sum up the form critical approach, we find it declaring that the individual gospel story has been composed by the early church as a product of faith. The church expressed the faith of the believers in the form of a gospel story, so that the gospel itself became a confession of faith. That means that the Gospel account does not go back to actual events rooted in history, but to confessional statements of early Christians.

For form criticism, the early Christian community was the cradle in which the individual story was born; and the early church, by teaching and defending the faith, gave shape to a developing story. Eventu-

---

[7]*From Tradition to Gospel.* London: Nicholson & Watson, 1934; p. 270.
[8]*The History of the Synoptic Tradition.* New York: Harper & Row, 1963; p. 368.

ally, all these stories were collected, put into a framework, provided with connecting links, placed within the gospel tradition, and regarded part of the Gospel. Bultmann, for example, claims that the story of Jesus sending forth the twelve disciples two by two to preach (Matthew 10:1 ff.) was born in a missionary setting of the Jewish-Christian community. This community gave expression to its faith in the spreading of the gospel. Consequently, it composed the story of Jesus sending forth the twelve disciples. Bultmann teaches that the early Christian community creatively produced the individual stories used in preaching and debate.

Some Observations

What shall we say about form criticism? Has this scholarly pursuit contributed anything to the understanding of the formation of the Gospels? Does the form critic use a number of hypotheses in order to arrive at conclusions?

Let us take the last question first: Does the form critic use a number of hypotheses in order to come to any conclusions? The answer to this question, of course, is in the affirmative. Anyone wishing to say something about the formation of the Gospels must work with a number of hypotheses. There is very little information about the period between A.D. 30 and 60. Anyone who wants to say something meaningful must make a number of guesses. However, apart from this rather obvious fact, the form critic has gone to many extremes in setting up hypotheses which have little, or at times, no foundation at all. Often, he merely speculates. And such speculation has not always been convincing; quite often it has led to skepticism.

To be a bit more specific: What kind of hypotheses does the form critic use? He assumes that a vivid narrative in the canonical Gospels, let us say the healing of blind Bartimaeus near Jericho, is the work of the early Christian community. The form critic has lifted the individual Gospel narrative out of its historical context and has fitted it into the framework of faith and proclamation (kerygma). To be precise: the form critic has made the early church the composer of the Gospel unit. The early church expressed its faith in the form of stories which it had composed, and it used these stories to proclaim the Word.

The form critic may construct such a hypothesis, but he has to show that the hypothesis rests upon some kind of foundation; he has to prove that there is some certainty for his hypothesis and that his reasoning is not merely speculative. Therefore, the burden of proof rests upon the shoulders of the form critic. He must demonstrate that a vivid narrative cannot have originated within the period of Jesus' ministry. He must show that the Gospel narrative is not a true-to-fact historical incident.

The form critic has received severe rebukes. By making the early Christian community the cradle of the Gospel units, he has virtually severed the tie with history. By placing the origin of the Gospel stories in the early church, he has severed the historical connection with Jesus Christ, the prophet of Nazareth. The form critic is rather bold in his assertion that because the early Christian community created the individual Gospel stories, we can learn nothing at all about the historical Jesus, except through the message of the early church — the kerygma proclaimed by the early Christian community.

We are told by the form critic that the early Christian community was a very creative community. When the Christian community heard an authentic word of Jesus, the early believers meditated on this word. They used this word to give expression to their faith. They developed the word and expanded it into a narrative, which, in time, found its way into the gospel tradition. Finally, an editor collected all these narratives and composed the Gospel.

A few things are quite obvious by now. First, the form critic considers the writers of the Gospels mere collectors and editors. Second, the modern student of the Gospels must find the core of truth in the individual Gospel story. He must do so by peeling away the several layers of details which surround that core; he must peel these layers much the same as one peels an onion. T. W. Manson, a British New Testament scholar, summed up Bultmann's attempt to find the core of a Gospel unit. Somewhere he wrote these remarkable words: "Bultmann proposes to give us Christianity without tears. What he gives us is tears without Christianity." Third, the early Christian church added many details to the authentic sayings of Jesus for the sake of catechetical instruction and missionary preaching. And fourth, the form critic asserts that the written Gospels are not founded on historical truth.

Reaction and Response

New Testament theologian William Barclay wrote a book in which he analyzes the studies of the form critics rather carefully. He makes a characteristic observation concerning the form critical approach to the gospel when he says: "What we have is not the earthly facts about the life of Jesus, but the Church's interpretation of these facts. What we have is not the record of history, but the witness of faith. What we have is not a record of Jesus as he was in the days of his flesh, but of Jesus as the Church experienced him to be in the light of the Resurrection."[9]

We may add to this observation that the form critic has overlooked the account of the "eyewitnesses and ministers of the Word," to whom Luke refers in the first verses of his introduction to the Third Gospel. Moreover, if the form critic asserts that historical truth is unfounded, he is rather negligent of the witness of the early Christian church recorded in the writings of the Apostolic Fathers. The early Church Fathers, among whom Clement of Rome, Papias, Polycarp, and Ignatius, had something to say in the last decade of the first century and the first few decades of the second about the formation of the four Gospels.

What does the form critic say to his opponents? He must give an answer to all the objections that are raised against his hypotheses. And answer he does. He is not at all perturbed by the rebukes he has received. He sees the issues clearly before him and, unruffled, he answers his opponents.

The form critic explains that he is not interested in the facts of history. Rather, he is interested in the faith which the early Christian community had in Jesus Christ. For example, says the form critic, the fact that Caesar Augustus was Emperor of the Roman Empire at the time Jesus was born is a mere historical fact; in itself, this fact does not call for a commitment. However, the fact that Jesus preached is an event which called for a commitment of faith on the part of the early followers of Jesus. That is important, says the form critic. Not in history books, but in listening to the preaching of the Word does man meet Jesus today. Preaching calls for faith commitment. Likewise, already in the early church, Jesus was not found in the annals of a history book but in the living faith of the believers.

Furthermore, the form critic asserts that the primary purpose of the canonical Gospels is not to give the reader an authentic historical account of actual events. If that were the case, we should have a chronicle of events accurately dated. Instead, we have a collection of stories and sayings. The primary purpose of the canonical Gospels is to present Jesus as a real Person. The Gospels present him as a living Person who calls man to faith and obedience.

What is the difference, then, between the evangelical view and the form-critical view of the Gospels? Concisely put, the evangelical view is that the Gospels are a reliable account of the life, death, and resurrection of Jesus because these events are rooted in history. The form-critical view is that the Gospels are the expression of the believer's

---

[9]*The First Three Gospels.* Philadelphia: Westminster, 1957; p. 26.

faith in Jesus Christ. These expressions of faith, composed by the early Christian church, are not used to prove history; they are used to preach Jesus to the world.

Serious Objections

Though the view of the form critic may seem justifiably true and admittedly acceptable, the adherents to the evangelical view have pointed out a number of facts which the form critic cannot afford to ignore. First, the passion narratives, as they are found in all four Gospels, are not single units but are given in a historical sequence. Although the four evangelists differ in regard to emphasis and detail, they reproduce the same pattern for these passion narratives. Therefore, it is virtually impossible to maintain that the passion narrative circulated originally in unit form.

Besides, the passion narrative is not the smallest part of the Gospels of Matthew and Mark either. In the Gospel written by Matthew the narrative comprises Chapters 21 through 28, and, comparatively speaking, the Second Gospel shows an even greater part devoted to this narrative. This somewhat brief Gospel account of sixteen chapters depicts the passion of Jesus in Chapters 11 through 16. And that is more than one fourth of Mark's Gospel.

The form critic does admit that the narrative about the suffering and death of Jesus must have been recorded as a continuous story. He qualifies this admission by saying that the passion narratives form an exception. But this qualification simply does not satisfy, because, if the passion narratives show sequence, we may expect sequence in the other parts of the Gospel as well.

Another fact which has been brought to the attention of the form critic is the presence of Jesus' immediate followers. The apostles were influential people in the early Christian communities. To be sure, the one hundred and twenty people upon whom the Holy Spirit was poured out on Pentecost in general, and the twelve apostles in particular, could not have disappeared from the scene. The book of Acts gives clear testimony: the immediate followers of Jesus preached the gospel as witnesses of that which they had seen and heard.

Furthermore, the preaching of the gospel, as Luke relates in the book of Acts, was not left to the discretion of the individual or to the choice and making of the Christian community. Luke relates that the apostles, under leadership of Peter, were fully in control. Even Paul writes that he consulted with the church leaders in Jerusalem concerning the preaching of the gospel. The apostles organized and directed the preaching of the gospel. "And the twelve [apostles] summoned the body of the disciples and said, 'It is not right that we should give up preaching of the word of God to serve tables. . . . We will devote ourselves to prayer and to the ministry of the word' " (Acts 6:2 and 4). The twelve apostles, as authorized eyewitnesses, were fully in control. They delivered the gospel as eyewitnesses and ministers of the Word.

Apart from the four Gospels, the rest of the New Testament shows that the apostles had a genuine interest in history. Though no one wishes to make the claim that the apostles were interested in writing history for the sake of history — the Bible is not a textbook on history — the student of the Scriptures does find a genuine interest in history on the part of the apostles: they reported and transmitted faithfully past events and discourses.

A third fact laid at the door of the form critic is the teaching method of Jesus. Two Scandinavian New Testament scholars, Harald Riesenfeld and Berger Gerhardsson, have focussed attention on the methods of teaching and learning in the days of Jesus.[10] They point out that in Israel, during the time of Jesus, the teacher (rabbi) instructed his disciples orally by having them repeat everything he taught. In the Hebrew, the word "to repeat" means exactly the same as "to teach." Students of the rabbi wrote down in their memories the instruction of their teacher: the disciples not only retained their master's teachings but also passed on the very words of their rabbi to the next generation. Students had to memorize in those days; for instance, the exposition of the Law might not be committed to writing but had to be transmitted orally.

In this setting, the oral Gospel tradition took form and shape. For the sake of clarity, we wish to emphasize that Jesus cannot be classified as a typical Jewish rabbi of the first century. However, the indisputable fact stands that he employed the teaching skills and methods of the rabbi of his day. Berger Gerhardsson elaborates this point and sees Jesus as the originator of the Gospel. Jesus taught the apostles during his earthly ministry. After his ascension and the outpouring of the Holy Spirit, the apostles not only proclaimed the words they had learned but also guarded them faithfully. The formation of the Gospel, according to Gerhardsson, does not find its origin in the creative Christian community of the first century; rather, the origin of the gospel goes back to Jesus himself. This is rather evident from the introductory sentence of the Gospel according to Mark: "The beginning of the gospel of Jesus Christ, the Son of God." Grammatically, the phrase

---

[10]H. Riesenfeld, "The Gospel Tradition and its Beginnings," *Studia Evangelica.* Berlin: Akademie, 1959.

B. Gerhardsson, *Memory and Manuscript.* Lund: Gleerup, and Copenhagen: Munksgaard, 1961.

"gospel of Jesus Christ" can be interpreted subjectively and objectively. That is, the phrase can be understood subjectively as "the gospel which belongs to Jesus Christ" and objectively as "the gospel which the evangelist dedicates to Jesus Christ." Though the one interpretation does not exclude the other, the subjective explanation is commendable; the Gospel belongs to Jesus Christ because he originated it.

Evaluation

How shall we evaluate the form-critical movement? One thing that can be said with certainty is this: the radical form critic fails to understand that not the early church produced the Gospel, but that the Gospel brought about the early church. The form critic maintains that the Gospel is an echo of the early church. The opposite is actually the case: the early church is the echo of the Gospel.

Rudolf Bultmann, at one time called the king of theologians, is considered a radical form critic. As Bultmann reflects on the formation of the Gospels, he sees the Christian community of the first century cut off from the apostles and existing in some kind of vacuum. Consequently, the life of Jesus is shrouded in a haze of uncertainty, and the emphasis is placed on the life and activity of the early Christian church. Thus, the New Testament professor of Marburg ascribes the origin of the Gospel narratives not to the so-called pre-Easter period — the time of Jesus' earthly ministry — but to the post-Easter period. Concisely, the early church produced the narratives.

What shall we say about the time element involved? The period between the ascension of Jesus and the appearance of the first written Gospel is somewhat longer than one generation. According to the radical form critic, during the period of A.D. 30 to 60 the vital connections with the period in which Jesus lived and died were virtually broken; the stories about Jesus, however, were composed by primitive people blessed with a high degree of creativity. Normally, the accumulation of folklore among people of primitive culture takes many generations; it is a gradual process spread over centuries of time. But, in conformity with the thinking of the form critic, we must conclude that the Gospel stories were produced and collected within little more than one generation. In terms of the form-critical approach, the formation of the individual Gospel units must be understood as a telescoped project with accelerated course of action.

To return to the one hundred and twenty people who received the Holy Spirit on the day of Pentecost once more: these people did not vanish but were active in many communities throughout Palestine, preaching the word which they had received from Jesus. In the letters of Paul, the words "receive" and "deliver" are technical terms referring to the transmission of a sacred trust. Hence, when Paul instructs the Christians at Corinth in the proper celebration of the Lord's Supper, he says: "For I *received* from the Lord what I also *delivered* to you, that the Lord Jesus on the night when he was betrayed took bread" (I Cor. 13:23). And in Chapter 15 of that same epistle, he uses these terms again: "For I *delivered* to you as of first importance what I also *received*" (v. 3). The form critic fails to take note of the faithful transmission of the very words of Jesus which the apostles delivered to the churches. In this chain of receiving and delivering, he does not want to see Jesus as the originator of the gospel tradition.

On the positive side of our evaluation, we do express our appreciation to the form critic. By means of his scholarly studies on the formation of the Gospels, he calls every serious reader of the New Testament to reconsider the period of oral tradition most seriously. The form critic invites the student of the Bible to study the background of the four Gospels anew. And that is an invitation no one may decline.

Oral Tradition

We can readily put the hypotheses of the form critic aside as mere speculation. But that does not answer legitimate questions. The primary question still remains: How were the Gospels formed? If we do not accept the form-critical approach, what answer do we give to the question on the formation of the Gospels? Though it is impossible to answer this question fully without the use of hypotheses, we do wish to approach the problem by looking at the total context in which the Gospel was formed.

Because the Gospel tradition arose in a Jewish setting of the first century, we do well to reflect once again on the teaching methods of the ancient rabbis. These rabbis relied on oral tradition in interpreting the Law. All kinds of legal injunctions, derived from a study of the Law of Moses, were transmitted orally and accurately from teacher to disciple, from one generation to the next. Jesus refers to this tradition when in the Sermon on the Mount he repeatedly used the formula: "You have heard that it was said." Disciples of the ancient rabbis developed the art of repeating constantly that which was learned.

The same procedure, we assume, was followed by Jesus and the apostles in transmitting the oral Gospel. The apostles had learned the words and teachings of Jesus by heart, so that they in turn might pass them on to the early church. The apostles did two things after the ascension of Jesus. First, they guarded the Gospel tradition which had been entrusted to them. And second, they disseminated the knowledge of the words and deeds of Jesus.

Although it is contrary to all evidence available that the apostles transmitted the oral Gospel in mechanical fashion, they did maintain a uniform approach in proclaiming the Word, together with their own human characteristics. As a matter of fact, the apostles did express their own feelings in their preaching, they spoke of personal observations, and acted on their own initiative. But one thing is clear from a study of the four Gospels, the book of Acts, and the Epistles, and that is this: the apostles limited their message to those things which Jesus had commanded them, by following a basic pattern. The apostolic message assumed a distinctive form to which the twelve apostles and Paul subscribed. Nevertheless, the apostles exercised their individual freedom in preaching the Word.

After the outpouring of the Holy Spirit, the apostles "were clothed with power from on high" (Luke 24:49). And one of the characteristics of this power was that the Holy Spirit taught them all things. He brought to their remembrance all the things Jesus had said to them. The Holy Spirit guided the individual evangelist in recording the message of salvation, keeping them from error, while fully employing the writer's characteristics, talents, and personality.

Of course, these summary statements concerning the origin and transmission of the Gospel are not intended to answer every question. They merely suggest the historical setting in which the oral tradition began, and they point to the work of the Holy Spirit in preserving the Gospel at the beginning of our Christian era.

III. REDACTION CRITICISM

Some thirty years after the rise of form criticism, scholars began to sense that form criticism as such no longer answered the questions which were raised concerning the formation of the first three Gospels. In other words, the discipline of form criticism had outgrown its usefulness. For more than thirty years, form critics had spent their energy on the individual gospel units without looking at the Gospel in its entirety. They had been looking at the proverbial trees and had lost sight of the woods. The Gospels had been regarded as mere collections of anonymous stories about Jesus.

In the course of time, questions concerning the authorship of the three Gospels kept cropping up: the simple answer that the early Christian community was responsible for the creation of Gospel material no longer satisfied. New Testament scholars compared the content of the three Gospels by placing it in three parallel columns. By doing this, they saw the hand of the writer of the Gospel, for behind each Gospel stood a different writer.

Because of this discovery, the somewhat simple solution that the creative community of the early church was responsible for the formation of the Gospel no longer satisfied. Form criticism began to yield place to redaction criticism.

Since 1920, the form critic studied the individual narrative of the Gospel as to form and use within the early church. By studying the individual units but never the Gospel in its totality, the form critic took a rather fragmentary view of his subject matter. That changed during the 1950's. Scholars began to study the aims and purposes of the individual evangelist. They were interested in seeing the man behind the Gospel; they had discovered that the person who wrote the Gospel of Matthew differed greatly in approach from the person who was responsible for the Gospel of Mark. Scholars were interested in the composition of the individual Gospel; they studied the theological motifs and themes set forth by the evangelist. In a word or two: they looked upon the evangelist as a theologian in his own right.

Representatives

The new discipline undertaken in New Testament studies is known as redaction criticism. Some wish to call it composition criticism. As the name suggests, scholars see behind the individual Gospel the personality of a redactor. They do not regard the redactor as a mere collector of Gospel units, but as a writer.

According to the form critic, the early church was the author of the single Gospel units. This anonymous community also gathered these units and composed the Gospel. But merely designating the community as editor of the Gospel did not answer the question why the individual Gospel reveals the hand of a theologian. Every Gospel discloses characteristics which point to a theologian who pursues a definite theological purpose. The redaction critic sees the personality of a redactor in the Gospel account.

Around 1920, three scholars spearheaded the New Testament discipline of form criticism. They were the German theologians Schmidt, Dibelius, and Bultmann. More than thirty years later, another set of three scholars spearheaded the New Testament discipline now known as redaction criticism. They are the German theologians Günther Bornkamm, Willi Marxsen, and Hans Conzelmann.

Günther Bornkamm was one of the first New Testament scholars who studied the theological themes in the Gospel of Matthew. He traced the doctrine of the church in the First Gospel. And as a result of this study, he learned that Matthew had interpreted the Gospel tradition which he had collected and arranged.

What Bornkamm did for the Gospel of Matthew, Willi Marxsen did for the Gospel of Mark. In studying this Gospel, Marxsen found that the Second Gospel happens to be the writing of a person who displays theological interest and skill. Incidentally, Marxsen coined the expression "redaction criticism."

What Marxsen did for the Gospel of Mark, and before him, Bornkamm for the Gospel of Matthew, Hans Conzelmann did for the Gospel of Luke. He took a fresh approach to the Third Gospel by looking at the author no longer as an historian but as a theologian. Conzelmann sees Luke not so much as a meticulous historian; rather, he views him as a theologian who, to a large extent, performs his work independently. This view implies that Luke when writing the Gospel was not historically motivated; on the contrary, Luke worked out a theological theme in his composition. Accordingly, geographical and historical details are completely subordinate to his theology. To be sure, these details do not have to be factual at all. It is theology that counts, not geography and history.

Methods Employed

Beyond dispute, redaction criticism has opened up a new method of studying the Synoptic Gospels. Earlier methods, such as form criticism, are outdated and will have to go into retirement. The new has taken the place of the old. For this reason, the discipline of redaction criticism deserves the full attention of any student of the Synoptic Gospels. Even though the discipline itself is relatively new, no New Testament theologian can afford to take the studies of redaction critics lightly. If he wishes to take his task seriously, he must stay abreast and take note of the methodology employed by these German scholars.

As the development of redaction criticism now stands, the discipline in itself is far from perfected. One indication of this is that the work performed by redaction critics thus far has appeared in the form of doctoral dissertations, inaugural addresses, and an occasional independent study. In the future, much work will be carried on. This will undoubtedly also affect the interpretation of the book of Acts.

How does the redaction critic read the Gospel? Let us look over the shoulders of Bornkamm and see how he reads the Gospel of Matthew. In his first work in the area of redaction criticism, Bornkamm takes the Gospel unit which deals with the stilling of the storm on the Lake of Galilee.[11] This incident is found in all three Synoptic Gospels, in Matthew 8:23-27, Mark 4:35-41, and Luke 8:22-25. In order to get a clear picture of the difference in presentation, we view the passages in parallel columns.

---

[11]G. Bornkamm, G. Barth, and H. J. Held, *Tradition and Interpretation in Matthew.* Philadelphia: Westminster, 1963; pp. 52-57.

Matthew 8	Mark 4	Luke 8
18. Now when Jesus saw great crowds around him, he gave orders to go over to the other side.	35. On that day, when evening had come, he said to them, "Let us go across to the other side."	22. One day he got into a boat with his disciples, and said to them, "Let us go across to the other side of the lake." So they set out.
23. And when he got into the boat, his disciples followed him.	36. And leaving the crowd, they took him with them, just as he was, in the boat. And other boats were with him.	23. And as they sailed he fell asleep.
24. And behold, there arose a great storm on the sea, so that the boat was being swamped by the waves; but he was asleep.	37. And a great storm of wind arose, and the waves beat into the boat, so that the boat was already filling.	And a great storm of wind came down on the lake, and they were filling with water, and were in danger.
25. And they went and woke him, saying, "Save, Lord; we are perishing."	38. But he was in the stern, asleep on the cushion; and they woke him and said to him, "Teacher, do you not care if we perish?"	24. And they went and woke him, saying, "Master, Master, we are perishing!" And he woke and rebuked the wind and the raging waves; and they ceased, and there was a calm.
26. And he said to them, "Why are you afraid, O men of little faith?" Then he arose and rebuked the winds and the sea; and there was a great calm.	39. And he awoke and rebuked the wind, and said to the sea "Peace! Be still!" And the wind ceased, and there was a great calm.	
	40. He said to them, "Why are you afraid? Have you no faith?"	25. He said to them, "Where is your faith?" And they marveled, saying to one another, "Who is this,
27. And the men marveled, saying, "What sort of man is this, that even winds and sea obey him?"	41. And they were filled with awe. and said to one another, "Who then is this, that even wind and sea obey him?"	that he commands even wind and water, and they obey him?"

The internal differences in these three accounts of the same incident are rather striking. But, says Bornkamm, whereas the accounts of Mark and Luke represent a continuous story, the account of Matthew is broken up by the inclusion of two incidents related to following Jesus. After Matthew has informed his readers that Jesus gave orders to cross the lake (8:18), he inserts two incidents which stress discipleship. First, a scribe comes to Jesus and says that he wants to follow him. Jesus says: "Foxes have holes and birds of the air have nests, but the Son of man has nowhere to lay his head" (8:20). Then another of his disciples says to him: "permit me first to bury my father." The answer Jesus gives is this: "Follow me, and leave the dead to bury their own dead" (8:22). Here we have a picture of the church and its members: the members question when they must follow Jesus and what it involves.

Concludes Bornkamm, "If this observation is correct it means: Mat-

thew is not only the hander-on of the narrative, but also its oldest
exegete, and in fact the first to interpret the journey of the disciples
with Jesus in the storm and the stilling of the storm with reference
to discipleship, and that means with reference to the little ship of
the Church."[12] Briefly, Bornkamm is saying that Matthew inserted
two incidents of disciples wanting to follow Jesus; after that, he has
Jesus teach the disciples a lesson in faith as they together cross the
stormy lake.

Now notice, says Bornkamm, that in Matthew's account the miracle
of stilling the storm comes after Jesus has rebuked the disciples for
having lack of faith. In the account of Mark, Jesus first stills the storm
and then rebukes the disciples. This is purposely put in that order
because Luke also follows the sequence which Mark has. Only Matthew, for his own theological purpose and theme, has changed the
order: *first* the rebuke and *then* the miracle of stilling the storm.

Only Matthew uses the expression, "men of little faith." Mark has
Jesus ask the question, "Have you no faith?" and Luke has, "Where
is your faith?"

One other observation is made by Bornkamm: in all three Gospels
Jesus is addressed by the disciples when he is sound asleep. Matthew
uses the word "Lord," Mark has "Teacher," and Luke repeats the
word "Master." In Matthew, the term is used to show respect to Jesus'
divine majesty; moreover, it is indicative of a confession of discipleship.
Surely, Jesus can be addressed in a number of ways, yet the very
choice of a particular word to address Jesus indicates the theological
bend of the evangelist. Mark and Luke may use the titles "teacher"
and "master" to express respect, but in the context of the narrative it
is Matthew who indicates the divine exaltation of Jesus by using the
word "Lord."

At the conclusion of the incident, Matthew says that "the men marveled." This expression is found only in Matthew. The other two
simply say that they, that is, the disciples, marveled or were very much
afraid. The expression "the men," according to Bornkamm, must not
be limited to the twelve disciples but to people in general. "The setting
of the pericope is thus extended, its horizon is widened and from being
a description of discipleship in which the disciples of Jesus experience
trial and rescue, storm and security, it becomes a call to imitation and
discipleship."[13]

What is Bornkamm saying by means of this interesting comparison
of parallel accounts? In a sentence or two, this: Matthew is an inter-

---

[12]*Ibid.*, p. 55.
[13]*Ibid.*, p. 56.

preter of the Gospel tradition which he has received, for in the changes which he brings about in his account, he expresses his evangelistic purpose (the gospel is *kerygma*). Thus, Matthew reveals himself as an independent theologian.

Geography and History

Willi Marxsen is responsible for and deserves credit for summarizing the trend of redaction criticism. In just a few statements he traces ʼthe development of New Testament criticism: first, there is the life-setting of Jesus in the Gospels; second, as the form critics teach, there is the life-setting of the early church; and third, as the redaction critics seek to show, there is the life-setting in the theological purpose of the evangelist.[14]

What does Marxsen mean to say in this summary? By the term "life-setting of Jesus" he means that some readers of the New Testament believe that the Gospels present accurate historical events out of the life of Jesus. The expression "life-setting of the early church" implies, according to form criticism, that the Gospels are a reflection of the life of faith in the early Christian community. And the words "life-setting of the evangelist" indicate the purpose and design of the writer of the Gospel.

Marxsen is not interested in learning what really happened and where it happened. Questions relating to history and geography are excluded because he wants to learn how the evangelist put his Gospel account together. The matter can best be illustrated by means of an example: the Baptist tradition in the Gospel of Mark.

The writer of the Second Gospel had the tradition concerning John the Baptist at his disposal. He did not want to record this tradition for the sake of historical interest but as an introduction to the preaching of Jesus. Thus, he took the tradition about John the Baptist preaching a baptism, was struck by the Baptist's similarity to the prophet Elijah, and was convinced that John was the voice crying in the wilderness (Isa. 40:3). How did the writer compose the first eight verses of Mark 1? He identified the voice in the wilderness, foretold in Isaiah, with John the Baptist, and in fact combined it with the tradition about the forerunner and the analogy to Elijah. He did this by prefacing the Baptist tradition by a mixed quotation from the Old Testament. He took the prophecy of Malachi 3:1 (also see Exod. 23:20) because it speaks about the prophet Elijah. Then he took the words of Isaiah 40:3. And these words constitute the quotation:

As it is written in Isaiah the prophet,

---

[14]*Mark the Evangelist*. New York, Nashville: Abingdon, 1969, p. 23.

Behold, I send my messenger before thy face, who shall prepare
thy way;
the voice of one crying in the wilderness: Prepare the way of the
Lord, make his paths straight.

According to Marxsen, this "backward-directed prophecy" was pre-
fixed to the Baptist tradition. Mark used these Old Testament passages,
applied them to John the Baptist, and repeated the words "in the wilderness" in the transitional verse (v. 4) which links the passages to the
Baptist tradition. (John the baptizer appeared in the wilderness, preaching a baptism of repentance for the forgiveness of sins.) The reference
to the wilderness, therefore, must not be understood as a geographical
location. Says Marxsen, "The wilderness is not a locale. We ought
not speculate as to its location. The phrase does not intend to specify
the Baptist's abode (not even in the most general way as adverbial).
Rather, 'in the wilderness' qualifies the Baptist as the fulfiller of Old
Testament predictive prophecy. Put in exaggerated form, the Baptist
would still be the one who appears 'in the wilderness' even if he had
never been there in all his life."[15]

When Marxsen comments on this particular scene described in the
first chapter of Mark, he intimates that the historicity and the geographical setting have no meaning for him. More precisely, he indicates
that the tradition of John the Baptist is only meant to be introductory
to the story of Jesus. John's story has to be brought to an end rather
quickly by means of the statement that John was delivered up and
put in prison — John exits and Jesus enters. The tradition of the Baptist
only serves the purpose of introducing Jesus. Thus, concludes Marxsen,
we do not have to think in terms of geography and history, because
Mark does not give us these details for the purpose of pinpointing
exact time and place.

Marxsen has a little difficulty with the very first text of the Gospel
of Mark. The text reads, "The beginning of the gospel of Jesus Christ,
the Son of God." To be sure, the verse would have been in place if it
had preceded verse 9, which begins the story of Jesus ("In those days
Jesus came from Nazareth of Galilee"). Marxsen interprets Mark 1:1-8
as preliminary material which to a great extent is parallel to the ministry of Jesus. Both John and Jesus were in the wilderness, both
preached, and both were delivered up. As a parallel, the Old Testament
quotation and the Baptist tradition belong to the Gospel, and thus,
says Marxsen, the evangelist could write: "The beginning of the gospel
of Jesus Christ, the Son of God" as an introductory statement (1:1).

What Marxsen does not say is that the Gospel from beginning to
end is the Gospel of Jesus Christ. He views the Gospel of Mark as

---

[15]*Ibid.,* pp. 37f.

a theological treatise of a first-century evangelist, who wrote and theologized for the church of his day. The evangelist was not concerned about geography and history; instead, he wrote theology. Thus, Marxsen views the work and purpose of the evangelist as follows: "The individual pieces are not only juxtaposed, they are also connected. The concept 'wilderness,' in itself geographical, is emptied of its geographical content; the reference to the 'delivering up,' in itself historical, is emptied of its historical content. Both are pressed into the service of a theological statement."[16] Mark is therefore an eminent theologian who wrote a theological composition for the purpose of proclaiming the Risen Lord to the church. This composition, called Gospel, does not convey information on time and place; it proclaims the Risen Christ. Significantly, Marxsen has entitled his book *Mark the Evangelist*.

At this point, a brief word ought to be said about Conzelmann's study on the Gospel of Luke. As a redaction critic, Conzelmann classifies Luke not as an historian who precisely establishes the record; on the basis of his work, Conzelmann regards Luke as a theologian. When Luke received the tradition of the gospel, he did not make it his business to record exact historical and geographical details. He reflected theologically on the tradition which he had received and then began writing the Gospel for the church of his day. He wrote the Gospel as proclamation. The Third Gospel, then, reflects the theology of Luke. Or, to put it differently, this Gospel reveals the purpose and work of the evangelist, not the purpose and work of Jesus Christ. We are dealing here with the life-setting of the evangelist, not that of Jesus.

Observation and Analysis

What shall we say about redaction criticism? Now that the pendulum has swung back from extreme left and is now, so to speak, on its way to center, should we be grateful to the German theologians who have studied the interpretation of the Gospels as redaction critics? What are the results to which they have come in their studies?

For one thing, we are thankful that the redaction critic looks at the Gospel in its totality. He has asked the simple question: Who wrote the Gospel? He no longer accepts the answer given by the form critic that the early Christian community is entirely responsible for the formation of the Gospel. The redaction critic, by comparing the individual units of the Gospel account, has detected the hand of a writer; he has met the evangelist. The redaction critic sees the personality

---

[16]*Ibid.,* p. 43.

of a redactor in the individual Gospel who is working out his own theological purpose.

In itself, studying the Gospel account in order to see how the evangelist worked is very challenging and interesting. Attention is now directed to the evangelist at work, and no longer does an undefined Christian community of the middle of the first century have a direct part in the work of composition.

The modern trend of looking at the evangelist as a theologian has much in its favor. No one is prepared to say that the Gospels are merely biographies of Jesus, and no one views the evangelists as mechanical recorders of past events. The writers of the Gospels do work with the gospel tradition theologically. They work out certain theological themes and in their work do disclose variation in purpose.

However, it appears that in his joy and happiness of discovering the work of the individual evangelist in the Gospel, the redaction critic has overreached himself and, consequently, is guilty of one-sided emphases. He has brought to light that the evangelist is a theologian who independently works out his own Gospel presentation. But this seems to be the only theme of the redaction critic. He does not take into consideration that the writers of the four Gospels also record history, that they also relate chronological and geographical details, and that they are apostles or followers of the apostles.

Marxsen, for example, says that the location for writing the Second Gospel is Galilee in the broadest sense possible. The Gospel of Mark was composed when Christians fled from the city of Jerusalem to the mountains of Galilee in A.D. 66 at the beginning of the war with Rome. Marxsen tries to show that the name "Galilee" must not be understood geographically, but theologically. Galilee has theological importance because it is the place where Jesus, according to Marxsen, had to work. Many times, Mark added the name "Galilee" not because of biographical interest and to be able to say: this is what happened and here is a true account. On the contrary, Mark wrote his Gospel out of theological interest. Mark wrote in order to proclaim the gospel, especially in his own community near Galilee. To put the matter in summary form: in the opinion of the redaction critic, Mark received the traditional material about Jesus and used it for his own theological exposition. He gave place names theological significance, and, living in Galilee, he took the word of the angels given to the women literally: "But go, tell his disciples and Peter that he is going before you to Galilee; there you will see him, as he told you" (Mark 16:7). That is for Mark the starting point, and from this orientation in Galilee, he composes the Gospel in a backward direction.

When Marxsen says that Mark was responsible for composing the

Gospel because there was no continuous, coherent "life of Jesus" at his disposal, we object. The apostles were in charge of keeping and proclaiming the gospel of Jesus Christ; an oral gospel circulated which can be detected in some of the speeches and sermons of the apostles, recorded in outline form in the book of Acts.

Furthermore, when Mark writes down the introduction to his Gospel in these words: "The beginning of the gospel of Jesus Christ, the Son of God," we wish to understand this statement to mean that the gospel belongs to and originates with Jesus; secondarily, that the writer attributed his gospel account to Jesus. We believe that the Holy Spirit stood behind the author of the Second Gospel, so that the Holy Spirit is the primary author and Mark the secondary author of this Gospel. We begin with the Holy Spirit and end with the Gospel writer.

Conversely, the redaction critic begins with the Gospel writer and ends with a proclamation which he calls gospel. The redaction critic says that there are gospel proclamations. We say that there is one gospel of Jesus Christ. We have four records of the one gospel of Jesus Christ. That gospel remains the same in every book because we speak of the Gospel according to Matthew, according to Mark, according to Luke, and according to John. We have the gospel of Jesus.

A second major objection to the methodology of the redaction critic is the subjectivity which he displays. He determines whether the names, places, and time references in the Gospel are subservient to the theological themes of the evangelist. Now, no one questions the fact that Matthew, for instance, develops certain themes in his Gospel account. Matthew works with the material at his disposal, groups many speeches of Jesus together, arranges topically many of the parables which Jesus taught, and quite often, in the interest of a theological theme, disregards the historical sequence known to us from the other Gospels. This is a fact, which no one wishes to dispute.

The point of the matter, however, centers on the factuality of reporting the historical events which took place in the life of Jesus. Though the Gospels are not presenting a complete biography of Jesus' life, death, and resurrection, they are nevertheless rooted in history. They relate the words and works of Jesus as spoken and performed in actual historical setting. The redaction critic, on the other hand, submits that these chronological and geographical references are significant only when viewed in the light of the evangelist's purpose. In a way, the redaction critic portrays the Gospel writer as a critical theologian, who would have no difficulty — anachronistically speaking — feeling at home in critical theological circles of today's seminary. Norman Perrin, in discussing Conzelmann's approach to Luke's Gospel, makes this telling observation: "What is more, it turns out that Luke himself was wrestling in his way with a problem which greatly concerns the theologians of today, namely the problem of faith and history in general, and the 'question of the historical Jesus' in particular!"[17] It seems that the redaction critic is foisting his theological mind upon the presentation of the individual Gospel and its writer. He wants to conform the thinking of the Gospel writer to his own critical thinking. And this, obviously, cannot be. The writers of Scripture, as Peter puts it, were holy men moved by the Spirit of God.

IV. AUDIENCE CRITICISM

In an age of technical proficiency even the computer serves the New Testament scholar trying to find answers to complex questions. J. Arthur Baird, chairman of the department of religion at the College of Wooster, Wooster, Ohio, has put the computer to work by checking out the Greek text of the Gospels. He wanted to learn whether Jesus adapted his teaching selectively to the audience he addressed. Do the audiences Jesus addressed tell us anything about the history of the actual words of Jesus? That is the question Baird posed. The computer did give him the answer and in a subsequent book, *Audience Criticism and the Historical Jesus,* Baird shares the information with his readers.

What does Baird do with Jesus' words, which he calls *logia* (a Greek noun which means *words*), and the audiences to which they were addressed? Quite a bit. He learned that Jesus taught selectively by accommodating his message to his audience. That is, the nature of Jesus' audience is very closely linked up to the type of message he delivered. To put it very simply, this means that anyone who interprets the words of Jesus must take careful note of the audience Jesus addressed.

Baird summarizes his findings in four major points. They are these:

1. The Evangelists are more careful to accurately preserve the audience than they are any other element of the logia context.
2. They agree with one another consistently to a higher degree on the nature of the audience than on any other point of comparison, including the wording of the logia.
3. A clear line of discontinuity must be drawn between the ideas and linguistic orientation of the Evangelist and that of the logia, setting the latter apart as a separate and distinct body of material.
4. A series of verbal, praxis, and theological patterns cut horizontally through the logia to such an extent that it is apparent there is a greater continuity and inner integrity to the logia than there is

---

[17]*What is Redaction Criticism?* Philadelphia: Fortress, 1969; p. 33.

to the obvious words, ideas, or practice of any single Evangelist, or of all Evangelists put together.[18]

These are significant points. For example, the last point is very telling for it reminds us of Paul's words "receive" and "deliver." The words (logia) of Jesus do not come forth out of a nebulous past; they show continuity; they were received and delivered by the apostles and the writers of the Gospels. Baird, calling the writers of the Gospels editors, makes this comment: "These editors are manifestly transmitting to us material that achieved its continuity prior to them. Furthermore, the fact that we can detect such continuity so often, and in such detail, demands a carefulness in the preservation of detail that is outstanding to say the least."[19] We meet a stability in the transmitting of Jesus' words which goes back to Jesus himself.

The computer serves the New Testament scholar well because it has given him the knowledge that the historical Jesus spoke the words recorded in the Gospels. Admittedly, the believer accepts these words in faith, taking them seriously, knowing that they were spoken by Jesus. Concludes Baird, "The historical Jesus was a selective teacher who spoke to people as they were able to understand, regularly adapting his teaching to his audience, and giving the totality, balance, and entire range of his message only to the twelve disciples."[20]

---

[18]*Audience Criticism and the Historical Jesus.* Philadelphia: Westminster, 1969; p. 136.
[19]*Ibid.,* p. 142.
[20]*Ibid.,* p. 173.

4. HERMENEUTICS

I. THE HISTORICAL JESUS

To raise the question: Who was Jesus? seems irreverent; asking such a question is to show doubt. But notice the question is phrased in the past tense: Who *was* Jesus? If the present tense were used, the questioner would express his desire to strengthen his relation to Jesus Christ. However, by asking the question in the past tense, we do so not to show or raise doubt about Jesus, but to introduce the modern theological trend known as the *Historical Jesus*. The question may be phrased in these words: How much do we know about the historical Jesus who lived in Palestine nearly two thousand years ago?

The theological trend labeled "the historical Jesus" is nearly synonymous with the name of Rudolf Bultmann. This New Testament scholar asked the question: What do we know about Jesus? But before we go into the trend itself, we wish to learn something about the man behind the trend, Bultmann.

Person

Rudolf Karl Bultmann was born in Wiefelstedt, Germany, in 1884. He was born the son of a German Lutheran minister; not only was he born in a manse, but he was born in a family of ministers. Bultmann's grandfather on both his paternal and maternal sides were also ministers. As a boy and young man, Rudolf heard theology from father and grandfathers; he was influenced by these men, so that it was but natural for him to seek a seminary training. At the age of 19, he enrolled in the University of Tübingen and later, in typical European fashion, pursued his studies at the Universities of Berlin and Marburg. He distinguished himself as a brilliant student — a fact which did not escape the notice of his mentors. Immediately upon the completion of his formal training he was asked to teach at the University of Marburg. This was in 1912.

He began his teaching career as a lecturer in New Testament studies. From the lowest rung of the ladder he gradually worked himself up. In 1916, the University of Breslau offered him a teaching position in New Testament studies. Bultmann accepted, received the rank of assistant professor, and stayed for a total of four years. After teaching at the University of Giessen for only one year, he returned to Marburg in 1921 and was given the rank of professor. Here he stayed until his retirement in 1951, so that he completed three decades of continuous instruction at the University of Marburg. Even in his retirement he kept on writing theological books and articles.

What makes the career of Rudolf Bultmann so interesting? Simply this. Throughout his career, Bultmann has tried to interpret the Gospels of the New Testament in terms of the twentieth century. He wants modern man to be able to understand the theological message and significance of the New Testament. Of course, this is commendable in itself, but hardly unique. Countless New Testament scholars have been and are doing exactly the same thing. However, what makes Bultmann's attempt unique is his method.

Method

When Bultmann says that he wants to interpret the New Testament gospel in terms of the twentieth century, he means this literally. The twentieth century for Bultmann is the scientific age: an age of birth control, heart transplants, and journeys to the moon. In this age of science and technology, the New Testament scholar cannot teach a literal interpretation of the gospel and expect modern man to believe such teachings as the virgin birth, the resurrection, and the ascension of Jesus. In this age of knowledge explosion, conceptions of a bygone age no longer speak to modern man; these religious beliefs must be reinterpreted in order to be meaningful.

Take the doctrines of the virgin birth, the resurrection, and the ascension of Jesus. It is scientifically impossible to have an infant born without the seed of a human father. The virgin birth of Jesus simply does not rest on scientific facts, cannot be verified, and must be regarded unacceptable. And in this age of medical advances, the New Testament scholar cannot set forth a literal account of the resurrection of Jesus and expect modern man to consider it as true to fact. It is simply impossible for a dead body to come out of a grave. Physicians may prolong life by means of a heart transplant, but once a person has been pronounced dead he cannot be brought back to life. Also, in this age of space exploration, the New Testament theologian cannot hold to a literal interpretation of the ascension and physical return of Jesus Christ. Modern man does not accept this kind of teaching any more. It is physically impossible for a human being to defy the law of gravity, to go above the clouds, to disappear, and thousands of years later to reappear upon the clouds and descend to earth in the same form and appearance as he ascended. Really, the facts about Jesus related in the Gospels must be reinterpreted for modern man living in today's scientific world. The literal interpretation of the Gospel is completely outdated and out of place.

Obviously, says Bultmann, the facts in the Gospels cannot be verified historically and scientifically. The Gospels do not mean to give us historical facts which we must understand literally. On the contrary, they reflect the religious faith of the first-century Christian community living in a typical eastern setting of the Middle East. Nearly two thousand years ago, the early Christians living in Palestine expressed themselves in religious concepts and symbols current in that day. They expressed themselves in oriental thought; they used symbols to express reality; and they had no intention of writing a history of the life of Jesus. The Gospels are nothing more than records of what the early Christians during the first century believed about Jesus. Comments Bultmann, "What the sources offer us is first of all the message of the early Christian community, which for the most part the church freely attributed to Jesus. This naturally gives no proof that all the words which are put into his mouth were actually spoken by him. As can be easily proved, many sayings originated in the church itself; others were modified by the church."[1]

Bultmann is of the opinion that the Gospels are not intended to be historical records of what Jesus did and said. The Gospels give the modern reader an insight in the religious world of the early Christians living in first-century Palestine. Now, says Bultmann, it is entirely out of the question to ask modern man to express his faith in Christ in the context of oriental thought of two thousand years ago. Modern man living in a scientific age must express his faith in terms understandable to his fellow man. The Gospels, therefore, must be interpreted anew for modern man. They must be accepted not as documents of trustworthy historical accounts of the life of Jesus, but as ancient religious literature of the Christian church.

How does Bultmann make the New Testament meaningful for modern man? He does not deny that Jesus really existed, but he questions the extent of our knowledge of him. Bultmann puts it in these words: "Of course the doubt as to whether Jesus really existed is unfounded and not worth refutation. No sane person can doubt that

---

[1]*Jesus and the Word*. New York; Charles Scribner's Sons, 1958; p. 17.

Jesus stands as founder behind the historical movement whose first distinct stage is represented by the oldest Palestinian community. But how far that community preserved an objectively true picture of him and his message is another question."[2]

Bultmann means to say that the early Christian community composed the Gospels; in doing so, it incorporated symbols in the composition to give expression to its faith in Jesus. These symbols are frequently mythological presentations of religious truths. Therefore, it is very difficult to determine what the true facts are when modern man reads the Gospels. What he has to do is separate fact from fiction. Modern man has to take the oriental symbols and religious myths out of the Gospel stories. Bultmann has a word for it. He calls the process of separating fact from fiction *demythologizing*. (The prefix *de*, like the word *dethrone*, refers to removing a specific thing from an object.) Bultmann takes the myth out of the Gospel story. What he has left is the message of the New Testament.

Now the word *myth*, for Bultmann, does not refer to an imaginary event but to an occurrence regarded by the early Christians as supernatural intervention. For example, they believed that Jesus was born because of a supernatural act of God. Modern man does not need a mythological presentation in order to be able to accept religious truth. What he needs is the message. The message of Christ is most important. That message can be applied to our scientific age, and that message can be understood by modern man living in a western culture.

We hasten to add that Bultmann does not say that the Gospels contain no history at all. There is some history in the Gospels, but that history relates to the teachings of Jesus. The Gospels, asserts Bultmann, are not a record of the deeds of Jesus. Because of this opinion, he comes to the conclusion that because the Gospels do not present historical facts about the person and deeds of Jesus, "we can know almost nothing concerning the life and personality of Jesus."[3] We do not meet the historical Jesus in the Gospels; instead, we read some of his teachings. We meet a divine Man who presumably lived in Nazareth, taught religious truth, and eventually was crucified under Pontius Pilate.

Message

Following the teachings of critical theologians of the nineteenth century, Bultmann makes a separation between the historical Jesus and the Christ of faith. The historical person of Jesus of Nazareth has little meaning for Bultmann. Instead, he places all the emphasis on the message of Christ. That is, the divine message is all important for the

---

[2]*Ibid.*, pp. 14f.
[3]*Ibid.*, p. 14.

Christian faith. To have a living faith in Christ the believer must hear the voice of the exalted Lord. Paul, for instance, refers to the voice of the Lord when he writes about marriage: "To the married I give charge, not I but the Lord, that the wife should not separate from her husband" (I Cor. 7:10). The living message of Christ is all important, not the story about Jesus of Nazareth.

However, Bultmann teaches that also the message of Christ, as presented in the Gospels, must be subjected to careful scrutiny. Many of the stories about Jesus are the product of the early Christian community. These stories ought to be removed before we can speak of the words of Jesus. According to Bultmann, the message of Christ provides religious truth but not historical facts. Of primary importance is the message which demands faith in Christ. Says Bultmann of the historical Jesus, "It is the appearance of Jesus of Nazareth and his crucifixion, events whose historicity is vouched for by eyewitnesses and by the tradition of which they are the source. All the same, it would be wrong to lay too much stress on this. For to begin with the historical Jesus was very soon turned into a myth in primitive Christianity."[4] The crucifixion of Jesus is a fact, but in itself meaningless. The preaching of the cross is significant, for it calls man to repentance and faith in Christ. The message of Christ is important.

The emphasis in Bultmann's approach falls on the divine Christ. Christ has entrusted his message to the Church, and in this message he calls man to faith. As can be readily seen, in Bultmann's approach Jesus of Nazareth is considered a mere man about whom we know very little. Whatever the Gospels say about this cannot be taken as historically true, apart from a few attested facts such as his life in first-century Palestine, his trial under Pontius Pilate, and his death by crucifixion outside the wall of Jerusalem. The rest must be regarded as myth and fable created and compiled by the early Christian believers. Thus Bultmann teaches that not Jesus of Nazareth but Christ, whose message has been kept by the church, is of importance.

In Bultmann's thinking, the message of Christ has been clothed in first-century oriental garb by early Christians. They used the religious myth of the virgin birth and of the resurrection to ascribe divinity to Jesus. But in the second half of the twentieth century, modern man must divest the Gospel story of its oriental dress, listen to the message of Christ, and respond in faith. Take for example the resurrection of Jesus. Modern man cannot accept a first-century myth coming out of a Jewish-Christian setting. History, science, logic, and nature tell him that people do not rise from the dead. Modern man takes the

---

[4]*Primitive Christianity in its Contemporary Setting.* New York: Meridian, 1956; p. 200.

myth out of the teaching on the resurrection, listens to God speak to him, accepts this word of God in faith, identifies himself with Christ, and rises to newness of life. That, in the opinion of Bultmann, constitutes the resurrection for modern man.

Application

In 1941, Bultmann wrote his essay, "The New Testament and Mythology," in which he introduced the new approach to interpreting Scripture. In this approach, he asserts that first-century concepts must be translated into twentieth-century concepts, if the preacher wishes to communicate effectively to modern man. If a man is to be called to make a decision for Christ, the New Testament must be presented to him in understandable and acceptable terms.

A preacher cannot ask modern man to believe in a fact. That is, man does not base his faith on a historical fact, because a historical fact does not demand faith. If the preacher says that modern man must believe that Jesus of Nazareth was crucified outside Jerusalem on Friday afternoon April 7, A.D. 30, how does this differ from believing that Julius Caesar was assassinated in Rome, March 15, 44 B.C.? Really, we do not believe that Julius Caesar was stabbed to death. We say, we know it as a historical fact. So, says Bultmann, we do not believe that Jesus of Nazareth died on the cross; we know it as a historical fact.

Then what does the message of the cross mean for modern man? How must the preacher today convey the truth of the gospel to the man in the pew? The preacher does not ask his audience to believe in a historical fact; he asks for faith in the message of Christ. Then, when man accepts the message of Christ and makes a decision for Christ in faith, he puts his old life to death. He breaks with his sinful past and thus, so to speak, he crucifies his old life. That is the meaning of the cross for modern man.

The resurrection occurs in modern man when he hears the proclamation of the Word of God. When he, in his existential situation, accepts that Word in faith, he rises with Christ to newness of life. In fact, when man accepts the Word of Christ in faith, then the crucifixion and resurrection coincide; they happen at the same time. Thus, when the Word is preached, resurrection occurs in the heart of man who accepts the Word in faith. When modern man makes the resurrection his own, new life in Christ is raised within him and flourishes. Concisely, crucifixion and resurrection are redemptive events in the life of the believer today. He dies with Christ and he is raised with Christ today. That, in short, is the meaning of the resurrection for modern man.

What about the resurrection of Jesus of Nazareth? Bultmann is very emphatic in his rejection of the historic teaching of the resurrection. The disciples of Jesus, "after their Master had been put to death by Pontius Pilate on the Cross, had seen him as one risen from the dead. Their belief that God had raised him from the dead gave them at the same time the assurance that Jesus had been exalted to heavenly glory and raised to the dignity of the 'Man' who would very shortly come on the clouds of heaven to set up the Reign of God."[5]

That Jesus died on the cross is a historical fact, but that he rose from the grave does not mean the physical resurrection of Jesus. It means that the disciples had some objective visions of Jesus' return from the grave. They believed these visions of Jesus' resurrection to be true, and they preached this message to the people. The death and resurrection of Christ are therefore much more than history; they constitute the preaching in which God confronts man to believe in Christ's death and resurrection.

When man believes, he takes up the cross and accepts the resurrection; thereby he takes up Christ's cross as his own and he experiences that faith in the resurrection of Christ is bringing him from bondage to freedom. Therefore, concludes Bultmann, the event that Jesus died on the cross is unimportant; so are the visions his disciples had about his return, interpreted as his resurrection.

Of importance is that man hears the proclamation of Christ's death and resurrection, that he believes, and that in the moment of faith he experiences new life. In the proclamation, which Bultmann calls *kerygma*, the believer meets the Christ of faith. Hence, for Bultmann, the Christ of faith is consequential; the Jesus of history has little bearing on faith because faith is concerned not with the historical Jesus but with the Christ who is proclaimed.

Evaluation

In the mind of Bultmann, we know next to nothing about the real Jesus of Nazareth who lived and taught in Palestine during the first century of our era. The reason for our ignorance is that the Gospels do not give us a religion of Jesus; they give us a religion of the early Christian community. We virtually know nothing about the historical person of Jesus, for the early church may not have preserved an objective picture of him in the written Gospels. We encounter many stories, many religious symbols, many legends, and many myths in the four Gospels. These religious stories, symbols, legends, and myths must be reinterpreted; they must be demythologized for the benefit of modern man.

---

[5]*Ibid.,* p. 175.

Two remarks must be made at this point. First, when Bultmann speaks of a myth, he is not thinking of some fanciful fairy tale, but rather of imagery used to express religious truth. Call it a symbol, if you please. When a cartoonist depicts a donkey and elephant in his newspaper comic strip, he conveys a political message to the American public. Likewise, religious symbols were used in the ancient world to convey religious truth. And second, Bultmann has no intentions of reducing the New Testament in size by removing myths. His method of demythologizing is a method of reinterpreting the message of the New Testament so that it is intelligible to modern man. The word *demythologizing* does not mean: removing the myth by elimination. Rather, it means reinterpreting the message of the Word of Christ. Demythologizing is reinterpreting. In Bultmann's own words, "To demythologize is to reject not Scripture or the Christian message as a whole, but the world-view of Scripture, which is the world-view of a past epoch, which all too often is retained in Christian dogmatics and in the preaching of the Church."[6]

As a liberal theologian Bultmann has raised an important question: How must we interpret the Bible in our scientific age? Evangelical theologians ask the very same question. Though answers and methods may differ, the question remains the same. Evangelical scholars struggle with the same problem — admittedly they come up with answers differing from Bultmann's approach. For example, Bultmann raises the question of interpreting such Biblical language as the heaven vanished like a scroll that is rolled up (Rev. 6:15). He asks what is meant by heaven above and hell (sheol) beneath. His answer is that such language belongs to an outdated world-view. By following the saying "Holy Scripture is its own interpreter," the evangelical scholar seeks to find Biblical answers to such questions. He finds that such language as "the gates of heaven" and "the scroll that is rolled up" does not convey literal information. Such language must be understood in context; then it becomes plain that the Bible does not intend to teach lessons in physics and geography. Nevertheless, Bultmann does ask the question about the world-view of the ancients and the view of the world we have today. There is a difference. And Bultmann, who has been among the first to point this out, has forced every student of the Bible to take a closer look at the Biblical text.

What then is the difference between the theology of Bultmann and that of evangelical scholars? The answer lies at their respective focal points. Bultmann has *man* at the center of his theology, the evangelicals have *God*. This becomes very evident in respect to the historical Jesus.

---

[6]*Jesus Christ and Mythology*. New York: Charles Scribner's Sons, 1958; pp. 35f.

Bultmann regards Jesus as a man born of Joseph and Mary; Jesus possessed divine powers because he lived close to God; he suffered, died on the cross, and was buried outside the city walls of Jerusalem. That, for Bultmann, is the life and death of Jesus of Nazareth. Evangelicals, however, ask why Bultmann has not included the resurrection in his view of the historical Jesus. The doctrine of the resurrection is the most important tenet of the Christian faith. What does Bultmann do with I Corinthians 15:14? Here Paul says, "If Christ has not been raised, then our preaching is in vain and your faith is in vain."

Bultmann answers this charge by saying that the teaching of the resurrection has a place in his theology because he teaches it. The significance of the resurrection lies in man who upon hearing the Word of God responds in faith. That is the resurrection. The resurrection takes place in the heart of man, whenever he turns in faith to God. Precisely, the resurrection is not something objective which happened once apart from the believer, but it is something subjective occurring in the very heart of the believer. Thus, the resurrection is not a past event which, according to the religious myth of the early Christian church, happened to Jesus. Instead, the resurrection is something here and now taking place in the heart of man.

All this sounds very interesting, but it is hardly convincing. The reason why evangelicals have difficulty accepting the views of Rudolf Bultmann lies in his approach to Scripture. He regards the Bible as a compilation of religious documents of the ancient world and early Christian community. He asserts that the Bible calls man to faith in God. For him, it is not the revelation of God rooted in history. He maintains that although the Bible may contain some history, it does not intend to give the reader factual information about events that actually happened.

What does Bultmann do with Jesus? He regards Jesus as a man who lived close to God. Jesus did not pretend to be the Messiah for he never said he was. Jesus never said that he would return to earth again. Jesus was a man.

Bultmann puts man at the center of Scripture; he rejects the teaching that the center of Scripture is God who reveals himself in Christ. He does not want to accept that God supernaturally enters history, that his Son was born supernaturally, that he died and was raised from the dead, that he ascended to heaven forty days after his resurrection, and that in the last day he shall return as the Judge of the living and the dead. This is the historical Jesus revealed in Scripture.

II. THE NEW HERMENEUTIC

For about forty years (from 1920 to 1960), Bultmann dominated the theological scene. In fact, during the fifties he was still called "the king of theologians." But this changed when in the sixties his influence began to wane. His disciples, the so-called post-Bultmannians, no longer wished to follow the theological track plotted by their mentor. Bultmann had been criticized all these years for reducing our knowledge of the historical Jesus to next to nothing because he proclaimed Christ as the basis of the Christian church. For many of Bultmann's followers, that break between the historical Jesus and the Christ of faith was just too much. They noted dangers in following the theological path outlined by Bultmann. By divorcing the historical Jesus from the Christ of faith, Bultmann came very close to being called a "docetic."

Now the word "docetic" comes from the Greek verb *dokein*, which means "to seem," "to appear." Historically, the term goes back to the second century of our Christian era when a group of people adopted the name "Docetists." They believed that Christ had no real body: he had merely *appeared* to people during the first century. Thus, Christ's appearance in the world was only an apparition. His body was not real, and his birth and his death were mere visions. We do not have to go into the history of the Docetists of the second century, but we do wish to say that the theological path outlined by Bultmann leads right into the camp of Docetism. And this was too dangerous a road for the disciples of the Marburg professor of New Testament theology.

The New Quest

The followers of Bultmann asked the question: Is it possible to see a relationship between the words which Jesus spoke on earth and the message of Christ proclaimed by the apostles and the early Christian church? If this is possible, they argued, we are able to say something positive about the historical Jesus. The first disciple to depart from the teachings of his master was Ernst Käsemann, who in 1953 launched the so-called new quest of the historical Jesus. In an article entitled "The Problem of the Historical Jesus" he pointed to the danger that if there is no connection between the historical Jesus and the glorified Christ of faith, Christianity has become a myth without historical basis.[7] Moreover, he asked the question why the early Christian church, which according to Bultmann had no interest in the history of Jesus, ever wrote the four Gospels. And last, he called attention to the fact that our faith in Christ wants to relate the earthly Jesus to the exalted Christ.

Many are the post-Bultmannians who have written on the new quest of the historical Jesus. Günther Bornkamm puts it this way: "Although the Gospels do not speak of the history of Jesus in the way of reproduc-

---

[7]*Essays on New Testament Themes*. London: SCM, 1964; pp. 15-47.

ing the course of his career in all its happenings and stages, in its inner and outer developments, nevertheless they do speak of history as occurrence and event. The Gospels give abundant evidence of such history."[8]

An American scholar, James M. Robinson, has approached the new quest of the historical Jesus philosophically. He contends that we should become fully acquainted with the life and culture of Palestine during the first half of the first century. Then we should learn to look at that life and culture through the eyes of Jesus. That is, we have to learn to understand the selfhood of Jesus. By living into the life of Jesus, the inquirer is able to understand the intentions and commitments of Jesus. Thus he can ask: What caused Jesus to speak and to act as he did? What Robinson does is to apply existential philosophy to the life of Jesus. He applies modern methods used in an existential approach to history.[9]

The new emphases stressed by the followers of Bultmann are encouraging. Nevertheless, apart from their desire to bring out the continuity between the historical Jesus and the proclamation of the Christ of faith, they differ little from the teachings set forth by Bultmann.

New Interpretation

In view of the novelty, introduced by the adjective *new*, the post-Bultmannians seem to have surpassed their teacher when they began writing under the title of the new hermeneutic. The literature which has appeared on the subject of the new hermeneutic is phenomenal. During the 1960's the post-Bultmannians seem to have heard the command: publish or perish. And publish they did. Apart from all the daring emphases expressed by the post-Bultmannians, the basic principles and methodology of Bultmann are much in vogue. We should not think that some disagreement with their master has led the post-Bultmannians to a conservative position on interpreting Scripture. To the contrary, some of Bultmann's disciples may very well be called neo-liberals in respect to the new hermeneutic.

What is the new hermeneutic? The word "hermeneutic" is derived from the Greek language; really, it goes back to the name of the god Hermes who was a messenger of the gods in Greek mythology. The Greeks had coined the word *hermeneuein* which means: to interpret. That is, the message which, for instance, Hermes brought in behalf of the gods had to be interpreted; he had to make the message understandable to the recipients. An interesting reference to Hermes is found in Acts 14 where Barnabas and Paul are called Zeus and Hermes by the

---

[8]*Jesus of Nazareth.* New York: Harper & Row, 1960; pp. 24f.
[9]*A New Quest of the Historical Jesus.* London: SCM, 1959.

people of Lystra. "Barnabas they called Zeus, and Paul, because he was the chief speaker, they called Hermes" (v. 12). Our word "hermeneutic" comes from the Greek expression *hermeneutike techne,* which is "the art of interpretation." Undoubtedly because of the German context in which the word "hermeneutic" is used in the singular, the term has also been adopted in the singular in English. Though this does not exclude the use of the plural "hermeneutics."

Should we attempt to formulate a definition of hermeneutics, we would put it as follows: "Hermeneutics is the science that teaches us the principles, laws, and methods of interpretation."[10] We are interested in the word as it applies to Scripture; therefore, we speak of Biblical hermeneutics or sacred hermeneutics. The adjective *sacred* in this expression sets it apart from general hermeneutics which applies to all kinds of subject matter that stands in need of interpretation. Sacred hermeneutics, however, deals with the Bible as the inspired Scripture. Already the writers of the New Testament indicate that they regarded the Old Testament as God's inspired Word. "Consequently, they took the historical material seriously, accepted its doctrine as proof for their own, perceived a divine unity pervading the whole, and in every way subjected themselves to its authority. The preunderstanding proper to our hermeneutics is belief in the divine authorship of Scripture."[11]

Sacred hermeneutics applies the principles of interpretation to the writings of the Old Testament and the New Testament. The interpreter who applies these principles in the conviction that the authorship of Scripture is divine accepts the Bible as completely reliable. His task is to build a bridge of understanding between the text and its reader. He elucidates the message of the text so that the reader may see and apply its relevance.

Hermeneutics and Exegesis

What about the new hermeneutic? What precisely is meant by this expression? Obviously the term must imply a departure from the old, otherwise the adjective *new* could not serve meaningfully as a prefix. Traditional hermeneutics has always made a distinction between hermeneutics and exegesis. These two words do not mean the same things; they are two distinct concepts. Hermeneutics is called the theory of exegeting Scripture and exegesis is the practice of the art. Hence, hermeneutics is related to exegesis as theory is to practice. The theory is the study of the rules, the practice is the application of these rules.

---

[10]L. Berkhof, *Principles of Biblical Interpretation.* Grand Rapids: Baker Book House, 1950; p. 11.
[11]C. H. Pinnock, *Biblical Revelation — The Foundation of Christian Theology.* Chicago: Moody, 1971; p. 209.

In the new hermeneutic this has been changed. The new hermeneutic has come to mean not the theory of hermeneutics but the practice of it — exegesis. Hermeneutics, in other words, means interpretation. James M. Robinson, in a chapter entitled "Hermeneutic since Barth," in tracing the meaning of the Greek word *hermeneia* says, "One significant aspect of the new hermeneutic is its return to this close association of hermeneutic with the *practice* of the art of interpretation, so that 'hermeneutic' can become coterminous with Christian theology as the statement of the meaning of Scripture for our day."[12] That statement of Robinson is quite revealing because it sums up the difference between traditional hermeneutics and the new hermeneutic.

Perhaps that difference can best be described by asking two questions: "What *did* Scripture mean when it was written?" and "What *does* it mean to me?"[13] The student of sacred hermeneutics asks the question: "What did the Scripture passage mean when it was written?" In sacred hermeneutics the threefold interpretation of the Bible is applied: 1. the grammatical, 2. the historical, and 3. the theological interpretation. The student using the principles of sacred hermeneutics first wants to understand the text grammatically; next, he seeks to gain insight in the historical situation in which the text was written; and third, he tries to explain the passage theologically in light of context and the rest of Scripture. Consequently, the student who implements these principles of interpretation gives an answer to the question: "What did the Scripture passage mean when it was recorded?"

The student of the new hermeneutic asks the question: "What does Scripture mean to me?" He is interested in making Scripture relevant to modern man living in a scientific age. And he wants to explain Scripture in terms of today's religious setting. Accordingly, Bultmann and his followers reinterpret Scripture passages, for example those on the doctrine of the resurrection, by demythologizing them. In their longing to be relevant they bypass the grammatical, historical, and theological (Biblical) interpretation. They look for an interpretation that is relevant. Clark Pinnock, analyzing the Bultmannian hermeneutic, pointedly writes:

> To take "resurrection," which has reference to the glorification of Jesus' body, and psychologically reinterpret it in terms of the "new freedom" the disciples felt, and then not to admit that one has made an important change, is intellectually dishonest. The dishonesty is compounded with absurdity when men are asked to

---

[12]J. M. Robinson and J. B. Cobb (editors), *The New Hermeneutic*. New York: Harper & Row, 1964; pp. 5f.

[13]K. Stendahl, "Biblical Theology" *Interpreter's Dictionary of the Bible,* Vol. I, New York, Nashville: Abingdon, 1962; pp. 418-432.

believe in a "resurrection" which never happened and to study a
text full of prescientific crudities.[14]

Criticism

A few things must be said by way of summary. The representatives of
the new hermeneutic have centered the meaning of Scripture in man,
thereby taking a stand opposite to that of evangelicalism. Evangelical
theologians consider the Bible to be a book about God first and about
man second. In the new hermeneutic this has been reversed, so that the
Bible speaks first about man, secondly about God. The point at issue,
therefore, is that the Bultmannians have made man the center of
theology instead of making God its center. Man makes judgments about
God and, in fact, reduces him to an object of critical studies. Man is no
longer subject to God and his Word but, with his new hermeneutic, he
has exalted himself above his maker revealed to him in Scripture.

The student of the new hermeneutic does not take the Gospel at face
value because he does not want to accept the history recorded there. In
this manner, all the followers of Bultmann deny the historicity of the
resurrection. They say that a physical resurrection of Jesus is simply out
of the question. And as far as the words of Jesus are concerned, they
also view them with skepticism. They maintain that it is very well possible that the words have been put in Jesus' mouth by the evangelists.
And precisely for that reason we do not have much proof that Jesus has
spoken these words. Only those words of Jesus which have no parallel
in early Christian preaching and in contemporary Judaism have been
spoken by him and are authentic. These words, say the students of the
new hermeneutic, must be regarded authentic.

The post-Bultmannian theologian is far removed from the position
maintained by the evangelical theologian. The evangelical exegetes
Scripture by approaching it as the inspired revelation of God. The post-
Bultmannian is interested in Scripture to study the sociological aspect
of Jesus' life; he tries to live into the life-setting of Jesus to learn why
Jesus spoke as he spoke and acted as he acted. Therefore, he does not
tell his readers what the Word of God says, but he conveys to them what
he thinks the words and deeds of Jesus mean. Conclusively, his study of
Scripture is man-centered; for the evangelical it is God-centered.

In their studies, the proponents of the new hermeneutic display a
rather negative view of sacred history. This negative view, however,
does not at all accord with the facts recorded in the four Gospels, the
book of Acts, the Epistles, and the Apocalypse. Eyewitness accounts are
drawn up as narratives relating to the earthly life of Jesus. These
historical documents testify that Jesus is the Christ. Why would the

---

[14]*Op. cit.*, p. 221.

church have accepted four written Gospels and honored them as inspired writings if the church had no interest in the words of Jesus and the historical trustworthiness of his life, death, and resurrection?

5. GOSPEL

I. CHURCH AND GOSPEL

When all four Gospels began to circulate in the early Christian church, believers began to reflect on the words and deeds of Jesus. They noticed the parallelism in the Gospels and attempted to form a historical conception of the life of Jesus. In other words, a harmony of the four Gospels would give the church a comprehensive picture of the life, death, and resurrection of Jesus. The first such harmony was composed by Tatian, a native of Syria, who about A.D. 175 transformed the four Gospels into a single presentation of the life and message of Jesus. Later, the name *Diatessaron* was given to Tatian's single Gospel. This name, which is a combination of the Greek words "through" and "four," actually means one Gospel through four Gospels. In later years other harmonies appeared. During the Reformation, John Calvin harmonized the contents of the first three Gospels in his commentary under the title *Harmony of the Evangelists*.

Creative Church

In earlier days, scholars spent their time harmonizing the Gospels. They tried to gather all the facts in order to gain as complete a picture of Jesus as possible. Wrote A. T. Robertson in 1922 in the preface of his harmony: "A harmony cannot give all the aid that one needs, but it is the one essential book for the serious study of the life of Jesus."[1] No longer are modern scholars interested in gathering chronological facts which may be gleaned from studying a harmony of the Gospels. They seriously question and even reject the historical trustworthiness of many Gospel passages.

---

[1] *A Harmony of the Gospels.* New York: Harper & Brothers, 1922; p. viii.

In an attempt to gain an understanding of the man Jesus, twentieth-century scholars have brought about a separation between the person called Jesus and the Christ of faith. They say that Jesus may have lived in Palestine during the first part of the first century, but we know little about him. The reason why we know so little about him is that the apostles and the early church changed and even formulated words of Jesus. They did this to meet the need of a given situation, or a particular setting in life. And because the words of Jesus have either been changed or even formulated by the early church, we know little about the person of Jesus of Nazareth.

The point which modern theologians try to make can best be illustrated by means of an example. We use the example of the word "church." Only in the Gospel of Matthew does the word "church" occur. Mark, Luke, and John do not have it. And in Matthew's Gospel it is found only twice. Once in 16:18, where Jesus blessed Peter and says, "and on this rock I will build my church." And the other time in 18:17, where the three steps of discipline are mentioned, "If he refuses to listen to them, tell it to the church; and if he refuses to listen even to the church, let him be to you as a Gentile and a tax collector."

The question is: Did Jesus really speak these words? Or to be more precise: Did Jesus use the word "church"? When Jesus lived on earth, no church existed. Jesus worshiped in the synagogue as is evident from the visits to the synagogues on the sabbaths. If he had expressed himself clearly, he would have used the word "synagogue" and not "church." The word "church" comes out of another age. When the church began to develop during the middle of the first century, the matter of church discipline became a problem. Something had to be said and done. Rules and guidelines were highly necessary. Consequently, the leaders of the early church formulated the words now known as the three steps of discipline, which were in time recorded in the Gospel of Matthew. The conclusion is that these words reflect the teachings of Christ, yet they are not words actually spoken by Jesus of Nazareth.

German theologians have a phrase for this development. They call it *Sitz im Leben*. Translated into English it means "life-setting." That is, the evangelist reflects in his Gospel account the life-setting in which he lives. He describes the life-situation of his environment. Thus, the redaction critic says that the writer of the First Gospel wrote these words within the context of the existing church and for the benefit of the church.[2] The church needed a message, lacked the necessary rules and directives, and had a need for a book on church order.

The form critic goes a bit further in his explanation of the term

---

[2]G. Bornkamm, G. Barth, H. J. Held, *op. cit.;* pp. 48f.

life-setting. He asserts that the teaching of the church as described in the First Gospel originated in the congregations of the early Christian church. The reader of the First Gospel, he says, must have an eye for the historical background of this Gospel. The Bible, or to be more specific, the Gospel of Matthew did not fall out of heaven. It originated within the context of the developing church living in the second half of the first century. Historical situations differ. The reader must see the difference between the life-setting of Jesus of Nazareth about A.D. 30 and the historical situation of the early Christian community some fifty years later. Jesus spoke in the language and thought of his contemporaries. The writer of the First Gospel spoke in the language and thought current in the second half of the first century. There is a difference.

Church and Theology

The explanation given by the redaction critic and the form critic sounds plausible and seems acceptable. The logic which underlies the explanation is convincing and compelling. Nevertheless, we are obliged to look at the arguments in the light of Scripture before we come to valid conclusions.

First, the emphasis in the explanation given by the critics falls on the church. That is, the church has given birth to the gospel. During the seventh and eighth decades of the first century, the church gave an account of the historical Jesus. The writer of the individual Gospel and the early Christian community wanted to say something about the life of Jesus on earth. Yet the writer of the Gospel and the church spoke in a contemporary setting in which believers gave expression of their faith in the exalted Christ; they composed and wrote the Gospel for the purpose of proclamation. They spoke as representatives of the early church and presented a picture of Jesus as seen through the eyes of the believer who lived in A.D. 70.

Directly and indirectly the evangelists wrote for the benefit of the church as instruments of the church. Take the evangelists of the First and the Second Gospels by way of example. Mark is the first to write a Gospel. He writes a short story, brisk and powerful, meant for personal use. His is a Gospel of action, not of meditation. Let us say that Mark writes his Gospel about the year 65.

Ten years later, Matthew writes another Gospel which is twice as long as that of Mark and which reproduces the content of Mark's Gospel very much. Has Mark made a mistake in writing his account? No. Certainly not. But the history of the church moves on. So much has happened in the ten years since Mark has written his Gospel that the writing of a Second Gospel is a compelling necessity. The church is confronted by enormous problems relating to the essence of the church. A gospel on the church has to be composed, which may be used as a guidebook for the early Christians.

When Mark wrote his Gospel in A.D. 65, he could portray Jesus as an outdoor man who roamed the hills of Galilee, spent the nights frequently alone in prayer, and even walked upon the waves of the Galilean lake. His disciples were afraid of him, says Mark. Matthew, however, presents Jesus as a rabbi who teaches the common people from the pages of the Old Testament Scriptures. Jesus, according to Matthew, directs the attention of the people to the Old Testament. In doing this, Matthew reflects the practice of the early Christian church of going to the Old Testament for answers to pressing theological problems. For this reason, Matthew has incorporated so many quotations from the Old Testament in his Gospel. These quotations answer the theological questions asked in his days. "No other Gospel is so shaped by the thought of the Church as Matthew's, so constructed for use by the Church; for this reason it has exercised, as no other, a normative influence in the later Church."[3]

The redaction critic differs from the form critic by saying that the evangelist has not merely compiled the theology of the early church. He is the interpreter of the gospel tradition which he has collected and arranged. By interpreting tradition, the evangelist, according to the redaction critic, can write his own theology. And he may do so by writing certain sayings which have no historical foundation, as for example, the sayings about the church in Matthew 16:18 and 18:17. These sayings reflect the teaching of the church, not the historical teaching of Jesus; they reveal the authority of a particular apostle, but do not go back to words originally spoken by Jesus.

This type of reasoning either from the form critic or the redaction critic fails to do justice to the historical foundation of the gospel. Either the church, in the case of the form critic, or the evangelist, in the case of the redaction critic, gave birth to the gospel. That is a half truth. The truth is that the gospel gave birth to the church and that the gospel rests upon a historical basis because Jesus stands back of it. The first verse of Mark's Gospel as well as the last verse of that Gospel are eloquent testimony of this truth: "The beginning of the gospel of Jesus Christ, the Son of God" (1:1). "And [the apostles] went forth and preached everywhere, while the Lord worked with them and confirmed the message by the signs that attended it" (16:20). The gospel, therefore, belongs to Jesus, who not only stands back of the gospel but who daily uses it to call his church into being. The present dis-

---

[3]Bornkamm, op. cit., p. 38.

regard for the link of Jesus to the gospel is brought out clearly in the second consideration.

Second, they who maintain that the church, either directly through a collector or indirectly through a redactor, gave birth to the gospel place the emphasis on the post-Easter period. They are of the opinion that in many cases it is impossible to speak meaningfully about an event which is rooted in pre-Easter history. The example of Peter's confession and the teaching of church discipline in Matthew 16 and 18 is a case in point. Jesus could not have used the word *church* because the church did not exist in the period before Easter. The concept *church* became relevant after Easter, in the so-called post-Easter period. Jesus did not establish churches throughout Palestine. The apostles did.

We object to this reasoning because Jesus has been given a second place. He has been forced to fill a secondary role. Jesus has become merely the man of the word and the apostles the people of the deed. They are important, not Jesus.

An equally serious objection to this type of reasoning is that the word *church* was already in common use more than two hundred years before Christ. The Greek translation of the Old Testament, the Septuagint, uses the word *ekklesia* (church) quite often; it is used to refer to the official meetings of the people of Israel. The word *ekklesia* is a synonym of *synagogue;* the words are used interchangeably in the Septuagint, and even in the New Testament such an interchange is evident. James, the servant of God and of the Lord Jesus Christ, writes his general epistle to the twelve tribes of the Dispersion. He writes to the persecuted Christians now scattered because of their faith in Christ, yet meeting from time to time for the purpose of worship. James writes about this worship service, in 2:2, saying: "Now suppose a man comes into your synagogue, beautifully dressed and with a gold ring on" (Jerusalem Bible). The word "synagogue" is the exact translation of the Greek original; the context nevertheless is that of the Christian church. During Jesus' ministry both words (*ekklesia* and *synagogue*) referred to an assembly at worship. Already at that time the difference between the two words becomes noticeable: the synagogue relates to the people of Israel and the church to the Christian community. Jesus himself is the first to apply the word *ekklesia* to the Christian church when he says "and on this rock I will build *my* church (Matt. 16:18). This is the congregation of believers in Christ. And this congregation belongs to him.

The point is that no valid reason exists for saying that Jesus could not have spoken the word *ekklesia* in addressing Peter and the other apostles. In fact, the evidence seems to indicate that Jesus did use this particular word.

Third, we need to consider the life-setting of the early Christian community and of the writer of the Gospel. Everett F. Harrison makes this observation: "Any writer, however objective, finds it difficult, if not impossible, to avoid reflecting his own situation to some extent. He cannot write in a vacuum."[4] The evangelists wrote the Gospel for the benefit of the church. Thus Matthew wrote his Gospel account for the Jews. He stressed the teaching that Jesus is King, beginning with the genealogy in Chapter 1 and completing this emphasis with the enthronement speech of Jesus ("all authority is given to me in heaven and on earth") in Chapter 28. Likewise, the other evangelists wrote their accounts to serve the interest of the Christian community.

However, the life-setting of the Christian community may never become the source for the sayings of Jesus. If the community, because of pressing needs, should have created certain sayings and should have ascribed them to Jesus, the very teaching of the historical Jesus would become uncertain. If we assume, for the sake of the argument, that the church or the evangelist has put sayings in the mouth of Jesus, we are forced to admit that the Christian community has composed a gospel of Christian teachings. Then the teachings of the exalted Christ have become important, while the teachings of Jesus, the prophet of Nazareth, become obscure. Joachim Rohde, in discussing the creativity of the Christian community, puts the matter in the form of a question.

> In the case of "community theology" in particular, should not the question be: "What sayings has the exalted Lord placed on the lips of his community?" rather than: "What sayings did the post-Easter community place on the lips of the historical Jesus of history?"[5]

The teachings of the exalted Lord, worshiped by the Christian community, is most relevant because the Christ of faith communicates directly with the believer; he places sayings on the lips of the community. Should this approach be correct, the New Testament itself would have to provide the evidence that such revelation was given to the church. But apart from the letters to the seven churches and a few other sayings this is not the case. What the form critic has done is to stress the significance of the exalted Lord and neglect the relevance of the historical Jesus. Jesus has been reduced to an unknown figure of the past; the early Christian community by expressing faith in Christ has become the creative agent as well as the source of the gospel. The church is first and Jesus second.

Teaching and Tradition

If we want to learn something about the composition of the gospel,

---

[4]"*Gemeindetheologie*: The Bane of Gospel Criticism," *Jesus of Nazareth: Saviour and Lord*. Grand Rapids: Eerdmans, 1966; p. 161.
[5]*Rediscovering the Teaching of the Evangelists*. Philadelphia: Westminster, 1968; p. 257.

the four Gospels, the Acts, and the Epistles do provide some information about the subject. Not that these sources satisfactorily answer every question concerning the formation of the canonical Gospels. Questions remain. However, sufficient material is available to speak meaningfully on this matter. Luke, in his introduction to his Gospel, informs his readers how he has composed his account.

> Inasmuch as many have undertaken to compile a narrative of the things which have been accomplished among us, just as they were delivered to us by those who from the beginning were eyewitnesses and ministers of the word, it seemed good to me also, having followed all things closely for some time past, to write an orderly account for you, most excellent Theophilus, that you may know the truth concerning the things of which you have been informed (1:1-4).

Luke draws up a narrative of the things which have been accomplished among his near contemporaries. He speaks of the things delivered by those who from the beginning were eyewitnesses and ministers of the word. He does not say anything about the church. What he does refer to is the tradition coming from eyewitness and preacher. The original Greek indicates that the eyewitness and ministers of the word form one group of people. These immediate followers of Jesus handed down the teachings of the things which had happened during the time Jesus was on earth. And they were busy in doing this because even the most excellent Theophilus had already been informed about the teachings of Jesus. The accent, therefore, does not fall on a creative Christian community but on the ministers of the gospel, who as eyewitnesses were transmitting the teachings of Jesus.

The early church put great stock in trustworthiness. In writing his Gospel for the benefit of the church, Luke underlines this concept in the first four verses, "that you may know the truth concerning the things of which you have been informed." Theophilus, who presumably was a high-ranking official in the government of the land, had heard the proclamation of the gospel. This oral proclamation is now verified by a trustworthy written account furnished by Luke.

The leaders of the early church did not have to formulate sayings of Jesus. On the contrary, they treasured the very words of Jesus because theirs was the task to keep and to teach them. Just as the Jews were entrusted with the oracles of God (Rom. 3:2), so the apostles were the guardians of the gospel of Jesus Christ.

II. WORDS OF JESUS

What can we learn from the book of Acts and the New Testament Epistles concerning the words of Jesus? Were the words of Jesus, kept by the apostles, faithfully transmitted to the hearers and eventually written down in the four canonical Gospels? That these words were recorded in the four Gospels is not in question. The point is whether the book of Acts and the various Epistles furnish any evidence that the tradition of Jesus' teaching was available to the early Christians. The question, in other words, is whether the early church was in possession of the words of Jesus before the written Gospels began to circulate. In order to answer that question, we must make some observations.

Prologue of Luke

First, let us look at the introduction of Luke's Gospel again. Concerning the events that took place during the lifetime of Jesus, Luke says, "just as they were delivered to us by those who from the beginning were eyewitnesses and ministers of the word" (v. 2). Luke calls the eyewitnesses "ministers of the word." The word *minister* is significant for it occurs only twice in the Third Gospel. In 4:20 we read that Jesus, having read from the scroll of Isaiah in the synagogue of Nazareth, hands it back to the *attendant* (minister, in the King James Version). The attendant was the guardian of the sacred scrolls stored in the local synagogue. He kept the Scriptures and on the sabbath handed the appropriate scroll to the person designated to read.

Notice that Luke does not call these people who were "eyewitnesses and ministers of the word" *hearers* of the word. Certainly they had heard the word from the lips of Jesus. But Luke uses the expression "ministers of the word." This expression points to the task, the activity, and the calling of these eyewitnesses. They had received the word from Jesus. They might not keep that word for themselves: they had to minister the word to others. The last verse in the preface to Luke's Gospel proves this point. In addressing Theophilus Luke writes, "that you may know the truth concerning the things of which you have been informed." These ministers (attendants) of the word had been active in transmitting the word which they themselves had received from Jesus.

Second, when Luke writes, "just as they were delivered to us" (v. 2), he means to say: the eyewitnesses have kept the Word of Jesus faithfully, and, as guardians of that Word, they have transmitted it to us. "By his use of this phrase Luke differentiates himself from the class of early witnesses and places himself in the second or a subsequent generation of believers. The phrase which he uses indicates that one class of people, who were both eyewitnesses and servants of the word, is meant, and we are probably to see the apostles as being comprehended within the group. In this way Luke is claiming to reproduce early tradition concerning the ministry of Jesus, and the verb which he uses (*paredosan*) may perhaps be taken to indicate the official manner in which the tradition was handed down."[6]

Acts of the Apostles

Next, let us have a look at the book of Acts. On the day of Pentecost the apostles proclaimed the Word in many languages, so that at the end of that day three thousand people believed in Jesus. What did these people do after their baptism? Luke writes that "they devoted themselves to the apostles' teaching and fellowship, to the breaking of bread and the prayers" (2:42). That is, the people were interested in being taught by the apostles. Of course, the hasty conclusion could be drawn that the people were instructed in the words of Jesus; they were taught the gospel of Jesus. But is this conclusion valid?

Luke, in the book of Acts, never calls the followers of Jesus *believers*. He gives them the name *disciples*. Whereas in the Gospel Luke calls the twelve both "apostles" and "disciples," in the Acts the twelve are "apostles" and believers in Christ are "disciples." A good example is found in Acts 9 where Paul returns to the city of Jerusalem after his conversion and tries to take up contact with the members of the local church. "And when he had come to Jerusalem he attempted to join the disciples; and they were all afraid of him, for they did not believe that he was a disciple. But Barnabas took him, and brought him to the apostles" (v. 26, 27). The term *disciple* is the equivalent of *Christian* in the book of Acts.

The word *disciple* means "learner." The Christians were learning the teaching of the apostles — they devoted themselves to the apostles' teaching. A few examples from Acts will suffice. "Now in these days when the *disciples* were increasing in number, the Hellenists murmured against the Hebrews because their widows were neglected in the daily distribution. And the twelve summoned the body of the *disciples*" (6:1, 2). The twelve apostles rectify the situation by appointing seven men of good repute to take care of the widows. They conclude the matter by saying: "But we will devote ourselves to prayer and to the ministry of the Word" (v. 4). These Hellenists worshiping in the church of Jerusalem were learning the teaching of the apostles, and because of this activity Luke calls them "disciples."

Another example: when Saul (Paul) wants to go to Damascus to persecute the Christians, they are known as "followers of the Way." Then Luke describes them further. Ananias and the other Christians at Damascus Luke calls "disciples" (9:10, 19). The Christians there are being instructed in the teachings of the apostles and therefore are learn-

---

[6]I. Howard Marshall, *Luke: Historian and Theologian.* Grand Rapids: Zondervan, 1971; p. 41.

ers. Not only in Damascus are the Christians called "disciples." Also in Joppa and Lydda the believers are known by that name, for they were being taught, among others, by Peter (9:32ff.). Characteristically, throughout the book of Acts the Christians in every place are called "disciples."

Did the apostles teach the "disciples" the words of Jesus? Did they transmit the teaching of Jesus? There are at least two direct references in the book of Acts which indicate that the apostles did exactly that. They taught the words of Jesus everywhere. When Paul at the end of his third missionary journey takes leave of the elders of Ephesus he mentions one of the sayings of Jesus. He says, "In all things I have shown you that by so toiling one must help the weak, remembering the words of the Lord Jesus, who *himself* said: 'It is more blessed to give than to receive' "(Acts 20:35). Jesus during his ministry had spoken this word and while Paul had preached the gospel to the church at Ephesus he transmitted this saying of Jesus. Now that he bids the elders of Ephesus farewell on the beach of Miletus, he merely recalls what he has taught in earlier days: the words of Jesus.

The second reference to the teaching of Jesus comes at the end of Acts, the last two verses of Chapter 28. Luke records that Paul was under house arrest in the city of Rome. He writes, "And he lived there two whole years at his own expense, and welcomed all who came to him, preaching the kingdom of God and teaching about the Lord Jesus Christ quite openly and unhindered." Though the church of Rome had been founded some years before Paul arrived there, inquirers who came to visit Paul in his home were taught the doctrine of Jesus Christ.

Pauline Epistles

What kind of an oral gospel circulated during the middle of the first century? Would the gospel which Paul or Peter preached be similar to the gospel, let us say, of Matthew, Mark, or Luke?

When Peter preached the gospel in the house of Cornelius at Caesarea (Acts 10), he followed the outline now known from the Gospel of Mark. And when Paul delivered his sermon, for example, in Pisidian Antioch (Acts 13), he preached quite similarly, so that we cannot speak of a Pauline or a Petrine Gospel. In outline form they preached the gospel of Jesus Christ as follows:

> God brought Israel out of Egypt, and gave them David for their king. Of the seed of David Jesus has come as Saviour. He was heralded by John the Baptist.
> His disciples followed Him from Galilee to Jerusalem. There He was brought to trial by the rulers of the Jews before Pilate, who reluctantly condemned Him.

He died according to the Scriptures, and was buried. God raised
Him from the dead, according to the Scriptures, and He was seen
by witnesses.
Through Him forgiveness and justification are offered. Therefore
take heed.[7]

A pattern of teaching was observed by the apostles and was accepted
by the Christians. Paul, in his letter to the Romans, refers to this
standardized teaching which the congregation in Rome had received.
He writes, "But thanks be to God, that you who were once slaves of sin
have become obedient from the heart to the *standard of teaching* to
which you were committed" (6:17). That is, the pattern of Jesus'
teaching was available to the church.

But do the letters of Paul reveal anything of the teaching of Jesus?
If we take the letters that were written first, we should look for some
possible indications revealing the words of Jesus. We must study the
letters which Paul wrote at the beginning of his Gentile ministry, when
the canonical Gospels were as yet unknown.

Presumably, the first letter Paul wrote was his first letter to the
church at Thessalonica. On his second missionary journey, Paul traveled
through Macedonia, preached the gospel at Thessalonica, went via
Beroea to Athens, and settled in Corinth. From Corinth, in approximately A.D. 52, he wrote I Thessalonians. In this epistle he refers to
the gospel of Jesus Christ.

What does Paul say in that first epistle? After the greeting, Paul
expresses thanks to God because the Thessalonians have become imitators of Paul and of the Lord; they received the gospel in much affliction.
Then Paul writes, "For not only has the word of the Lord sounded forth
from you in Macedonia and Achaia, but your faith in God has gone
forth everywhere, so that we need not say anything" (1:8). That is
significant.

The Thessalonians, Paul says, are now proclaiming the word of the
Lord which we have taught them. When Paul and his fellow missionaries taught the word of the Lord, they did not leave pocket New Testaments behind for all the believers in Thessalonica. Teaching occurred
orally, and the words of Jesus had to be memorized. Teaching for Paul
and the church at Thessalonica was a matter of receiving and delivering; it was the transmission of a tradition, quite often referred to as
paradosis (the Greek word for handing down). In commenting on the
oral tradition in Paul's letters to the church at Thessalonica, Reinier
Schippers says, "There are no other epistles of Paul in which the theme

---

[7]C. H. Dodd, *The Apostolic Preaching and its Developments*. London: Hodder &
Stoughton, 1950 (6th printing); p. 29.

of *paradosis* is so frequently under discussion as those which he wrote to the Thessalonians."[8]

Paul mentions the theme of tradition again in Chapter 2 of the first epistle. "And we also thank God constantly for this, that when you *received* the word of God which you *heard* from us, you accepted it not as the word of men but as what it really is, the word of God, which is at work in you believers" (v. 13). The verses which follow explicate this "word of God" because they show a remarkable resemblance to the words of Jesus recorded in Matthew 23:29-36.

Comparing the persecution which the Thessalonians had suffered to that of the churches in Judea, Paul writes that the Jews

> killed both the Lord Jesus, and the prophets, and drove us out, and displease God and oppose all men, by hindering us from speaking to the Gentiles that they may be saved — so as always to fill up the measure of their sins. But God's wrath has come upon them at last (vv. 15 and 16).

Though the passage of the speech of Jesus, in Matthew 23, is too long a few select verses reveal the similarity.

> Thus you witness against yourselves, that you are sons of those who murdered the prophets. Fill up, then, the measure of your fathers. Therefore I send you prophets and wise men and scribes, some of whom you will kill and crucify, and some you will scourge in your synagogues and persecute from town to town. Truly, I say to you, all this will come upon this generation (vv. 31ff.)

The same key words are found in both passages; the words: kill, prophets, persecute, and fill up. All these words appear in the same sequence of thought: killing the prophets, driving them out, and filling up the wrath of God coming upon them. Paul also speaks of the death of Jesus by saying that the Jews killed the Lord Jesus and the prophets. The verb "to kill" is used by Jesus when he foretells his death, for example in Matthew 16:21 "and be killed." Jesus constantly instructed his followers about his imminent death. And in his instruction he used the verb "to kill" which is also found in I Thessalonians 2:15.

We have to keep in mind that Paul wrote this letter in approximately A.D. 52, and that at that time the Gospels of Matthew, Mark, and Luke were not yet in circulation. In his epistles to the Thessalonians, Paul unmistakably relies on the teaching of Jesus. As he himself indicates, he is handing down a tradition from the same source. "Where else would the apostle have derived such data other than from the traditions as he found them in the primitive church?"[9] Paul preached the gospel of Jesus, which he places on the same level as the Old Testament

[8]"Pre-Synoptic Tradition in I Thessalonians II 13-16," *Novum Testamentum* 8 (2-4, 1966); p. 224.
[9]*Ibid.*, p. 223.

Scriptures; he not only refers to this gospel as the word of the Lord, but as the word of God. In his first letter to the Thessalonians, Paul indicates that the source of "his gospel" lies not in man ("you accepted it not as the word of men"), but in the Lord. In short, the source is divine.

Because I Thessalonians is an early epistle from the hand of Paul, we should pay close attention to the term *tradition*. The concept *tradition* comes to expression most in the letters to the church at Thessalonica: those two epistles take precedence over all the other Pauline Epistles in the use of this theme. Furthermore, throughout the Thessalonian epistles Paul reminds his readers of the commands he gave them. He calls attention to earlier instructions: "Do you not remember, that when I was still with you I told you this?" (II Thess. 2:5), and "For even when we were with you, we gave you this command" (II Thess. 3:10).

What does this emphasis on the word and concept *tradition* indicate? For one thing, it shows that Paul had received the sayings of Jesus. On his missionary journeys, he diligently instructed believers, so that they became the recipients of the tradition, known as the word of the Lord. Paul was the teacher and the believers were his disciples, the learners. As Paul had received the gospel of Jesus and delivered it to the churches, so the believers accepted the tradition from Paul and in turn passed it on to their fellow men.

Paul taught in rabbinical fashion. That is, besides transmitting the word of the Lord, he also showed that this word must be obeyed in life. Therefore he says, "as you have an example in us." By obedience he means that the hearers of the words of Jesus must in turn become teachers: they must transmit the sayings of the Lord. And this is exactly what the believers in the church of Thessalonica did. In I Thessalonians 1 Paul commends them highly. "And you became imitators of us and of the Lord, for you received the word in much affliction, with joy inspired by the Holy Spirit; so that you became an example to all the believers in Macedonia and in Achaia" (vv. 6, 7). The believers in Thessalonica became the sounding board of the gospel of Jesus, for the good news was heard throughout Macedonia and Greece.

A chain in the theme "receive and deliver" becomes apparent: from Jesus to Paul, from Paul to the Thessalonians, and from the Thessalonians to the people in Macedonia and Greece. This chain embodies two characteristics: example and instruction. Jesus is the example who gives the apostles instructions; Paul in obeying God becomes an example himself to the Thessalonians, who receive Paul's command; and they in turn become examples to the inhabitants of Macedonia and Greece.

Epistle of James

The Epistle of James is commonly believed to date from the same time as I Thessalonians, if not five years earlier. The point is that the writer of this epistle could not rely on any written Gospels because they did not exist at that time. And yet throughout James' epistle, references and allusions — not to speak of verbal similarities — to the canonical Gospels are very frequent. "This epistle contains more verbal reminiscences of the teaching of Jesus than all the other apostolic writings taken together."[10]

The epistle reveals so many similarities to the Sermon on the Mount that it is to a great extent an echo of Chapters 5 through 7 of Matthew's Gospel. However, this Gospel was not yet composed when James wrote his epistle. In other words, James and Matthew rely on the same source when they write their documents.

Though the wording may not be identical, the thought between James' epistle and the Sermon on the Mount is striking. A few examples illustrate the point. James writes, "And let steadfastness have its full effect, that you may be perfect and complete, lacking in nothing" (1:4). Jesus says, "You, therefore, must be perfect, as your heavenly Father is perfect" (Matt. 5:48). Instructing the rich, James warns, "Your riches have rotted and your garments are moth-eaten. Your gold and silver have rusted, and their rust will be evidence against you and will eat your flesh like fire. You have laid up treasure for the last days" (5:2, 3). Unmistakably this is an echo of Jesus' word, "Do not lay up for yourselves treasures on earth, where moth and rust consume and where thieves break in and steal, but lay up for yourselves treasures in heaven, where neither moth nor rust consumes and where thieves do not break in and steal" (Matt. 6:19, 20).

James repeats a saying of Jesus nearly verbatim. In fact, someone reading or hearing the saying may not readily be able to determine whether it comes from the Sermon on the Mount or from James' epistle.

Matthew 5:34-37	*James 5:12*
But I say to you, Do not swear at all, either by heaven, for it is the throne of God, or by the earth, for it is his footstool, or by Jerusalem, for it is the city of the great King. And do not swear by your head, for you cannot make one hair white or black. Let what you say be simply "Yes" or "No"; anything more than this comes from evil.	But above all, my brethren, do not swear, either by heaven or by earth or with any other oath,

but let your yes be yes and your no be no, that you may not fall under condemnation. |

---

[10]A. Ross, *The Epistles of James and John*. Grand Rapids: Eerdmans, 1960; p. 16.

The entire epistle is permeated with the words of Jesus. Moreover, the writer presumes a knowledge of these words on the part of his readers. Thus, he is not teaching his readers something new; he is merely reminding them of the teaching they have received at an earlier time.

Tradition

We wish to draw the conclusion that the whole body of Jesus' teaching was available to the apostles and, through them, to the early Christians before the canonical Gospels were written. The apostles' teaching (Acts 2:42) consisted of a pattern which comprised the facts about the Lord Jesus Christ (Acts 28:31). That is, the apostles proclaimed the good news by teaching the people the life, words, and doctrine of Jesus. They developed this teaching, they gave it form and shape, they standardized it. One of the reasons why the apostles remained such a long time in Jerusalem after the outpouring of the Holy Spirit on Pentecost was to formulate the so-called apostles' teaching.

The apostles were responsible for delivering the facts concerning Jesus. When believers, such as Paul, came to Jerusalem, they could confer with one of the leaders and receive the tradition. "When did Paul 'receive' the tradition of the death and resurrection of Christ? His conversion can, on his own showing, be dated not later than about A.D. 33-34. His first visit to Jerusalem was three years after this (possibly just over two years on our exclusive reckoning); at the utmost, therefore, not more than seven years after the Crucifixion. At that time he stayed with Peter for a fortnight, and we may presume they did not spend all the time talking about the weather. After that he had no direct contact with the primitive church for fourteen years, that is to say, almost down to the period to which our epistles belong, and it is difficult to see how he could during this time have had any opportunity of further instruction in the apostolic traditions."[11]

The formulation of the apostles' teaching was a communal matter. Paul, who could not say that he had followed the Lord Jesus Christ from the time of his baptism by John to the day of his ascension, received the apostolic tradition from Peter (Gal. 1:18). After preaching to the Gentiles, he consulted with the apostles in Jerusalem about the gospel which he preached. "Then after fourteen years I went up to Jerusalem with Barnabas, taking Titus along with me. I went up by revelation; and I laid before them (but privately before those who were of repute) the gospel which I preach among the Gentiles, lest somehow I should be running or had run in vain" (Gal. 2:1, 2).

---

[11]Dodd, *op. cit.*, p. 16.

Paul does not imply that he had deviated from the tradition of Jesus' words; he means to say that the gospel in its proclamation is not a private concern but is a matter of communal action and interest. Therefore, an apostle had to work in consultation with the rest of the apostles.

Of course, every apostle used his own talents in the proclamation of the gospel of Jesus. Paul, for example, in a number of his epistles personalizes the gospel by calling it either "my gospel" or "our gospel." The apostles, even though they had standardized the tradition of Jesus' words, did enjoy the freedom to preach the gospel of Jesus as they saw fit. Nevertheless, the basic framework of the facts concerning Jesus remained the same.

The tradition of the apostles' teaching was transmitted orally for the first few decades after Pentecost. The apostles instructed the believers (disciples) and memorization was the learning process of that age. Studying the methodology of that century, we find that the disciples memorized verbatim what their instructors taught. Emil Schürer, the eminent authority on the history of the Jewish people, wrote, "The instruction consisted of an indefatigable continuous exercise of the memory. . . . The teacher was obliged to repeat his matter again and again with his pupils. Hence the Rabbinic diction 'to repeat' means exactly the same as 'to teach.' "[12]

Admittedly, Jesus and the apostles may not be regarded as typical Jewish rabbis. However, in his oral teaching, Jesus employed the same method. The phrase "and he opened his mouth and taught" is familiar. Also, Jesus' immediate followers taught orally.

Besides, a few of his disciples knew how to write, so that written accounts began to appear before Luke contemplated writing his account. The opening words of Luke's Gospel refer to this. "Inasmuch as many have undertaken to compile a narrative of the things which have been accomplished." Luke does not indicate how many accounts circulated at the time of his writing, nor does he imply that the accounts were inaccurate. He says that because others have written he also has composed an orderly account.

In the tradition from the oral gospel to the written, the authenticity of Jesus' words remained the same. Joachim Jeremias, in a study on the tradition of the sayings of Jesus, draws up the following criterion: "In the synoptic tradition it is the inauthenticity, and not the authenticity, of the sayings of Jesus that must be demonstrated."[13] His conclusion is that the evidence from a linguistic and stylistic point of view testifies

---

[12]*A History of the Jewish People in the Time of Jesus Christ.* Edinburgh: T. & T. Clark, 1885; Division II, Vol. I. p. 324.
[13]*New Testament Theology.* New York: Charles Scribner's Sons, 1971; p. 37.

to the faithfulness of the sayings of Jesus recorded in the Gospels of Matthew, Mark, and Luke.

Authority

At least at two places the New Testament epistles indicate that the apostolic teaching is authoritative. The first indication is in II Peter 3:2, where the writer in a word of exhortation says, "that you should remember the predictions of the holy prophets and the commandment of the Lord and Savior through your apostles." The apostles are put on the same level as the holy prophets; besides they are designated as agents of the Lord Jesus Christ. It is also noteworthy that they are called *your* apostles. That is, the apostles known to the readers speak as ambassadors in behalf of the Lord Jesus Christ and therefore are endowed with the same measure of authority.

The second reference is found in Jude 17. "But you must remember, beloved, the predictions of the apostles of our Lord Jesus Christ." If this letter was written in the period between A.D. 70 to 90, many of the apostles had already died. Therefore, Jude gives the exhortation to remember the words of the apostles, who spoke with the authority of the Lord Jesus Christ.

Also the writings of the Apostolic Fathers indicate the same respect for the apostolic teaching. For instance, Clement of Rome, writing his letter to the church at Corinth in the year 96, says, "The Apostles received the Gospel for us from the Lord Jesus Christ; Jesus Christ was sent forth from God. So then Christ is sent from God, and the Apostles are from Christ. Both therefore came of the will of God in the appointed order" (I Clem. 42:1, 2).[14] Likewise his contemporary, Ignatius, writing a letter to the church at Magnesia which was located a few miles south of Ephesus, makes the same comment: "Do your diligence therefore that ye be confirmed in the ordinances of the Lord and of the Apostles" (13:1).[15]

Church leaders at the end of the first century regarded the apostles' teachings as authoritative because the apostles faithfully brought the gospel of Jesus. Moreover, they accorded the apostles the same respect and reverence as the prophets who composed the Old Testament Scriptures. Conclusively, they regarded the apostles as mouthpieces of the Lord Jesus Christ. What the apostles said and wrote to the early church was authoritative because behind them stood Jesus Christ himself.

---

[14] J. B. Lightfoot, *The Apostolic Fathers.* Grand Rapids: Baker, 1962; p. 31.
[15] *Ibid.,* p. 71.

6. THE GOSPELS

I. MATTHEW

Authorship

What has happened to the popular idea that the Apostle Matthew is the author of the First Gospel? Many scholars have discredited the idea that Matthew is the author. They point out a number of objections, such as the close similarity between the text of Matthew and that of Mark, which seems to indicate that Matthew depended on Mark. They say that if the writer of Matthew's Gospel were an eyewitness, he would not have relied upon an account written not by an apostle but by a follower of the apostles. He would not depend on the account of Mark; he would write his own. Therefore, they claim, the First Gospel must have been written by someone other than the Apostle Matthew.

However, this does not mean that Matthew, the apostle, did not have a hand in the early formation of the Gospel. From the beginning of the second century comes an interesting note. Papias, bishop of Hierapolis, near Laodicea in Asia Minor, wrote at that time that "Matthew compiled the oracles (Greek *logia*) in the Hebrew language; but everyone interpreted them as he was able."[1] If the word "oracles" is interpreted to mean "gospel," Papias must be considered the first witness who links the Apostle Matthew to the First Gospel. The question, however, is how the word "oracles" (*logia*) was understood by Papias and other church leaders during the first few centuries.

Some scholars are of the opinion that these sayings may have comprised some kind of book of collected sayings of Jesus, much the same as the Gospel of Thomas. They surmise that a converted rabbi, in later years, took these sayings together with the Gospel of Mark, added the teachings of the developing Christian church, and wrote the Gospel of

---

[1]Eusebius, *Ecclesiastical History* III, 39, 16. Loeb Classical Library.

Matthew. That is, the sources for the writing of the canonical Gospel of Matthew are the oracles written by Matthew in the Hebrew language, the Gospel of Mark, and some add, a source known as M which contained material found only in the First Gospel.

Other scholars regard the term *oracles* to mean gospel because the context in which the term is found seems to indicate that this is the meaning. Papias also mentions the Gospel of Mark, which he describes as the record of "the things either said or done by the Lord." These things are the oracles of the Lord, he says.[2] If he mentions the word *oracles* in connection with the Gospel of Mark and then continues to talk about the oracles which Matthew compiled, scholars draw the conclusion that the term *logia* is equivalent to the Gospel. The fact remains, nevertheless, that this Gospel was written in the "Hebrew" language.

Looking at the origin and structure of Matthew's Gospel from another direction, G. D. Kilpatrick argues that this Gospel must have originated in the worship services of the early church. He asserts that it was written for liturgical and catechetical purposes, that "the Gospel was compiled out of materials which had already been read and expounded in the services of the Church and that the evangelist composed it to serve this purpose more fully in the future. . . . Another proof of its success lies in its constant and preferential use by the Church."[3]

Krister Stendahl embroiders still further on this pattern by pointing out that within the early church there may have been a school. Says Stendahl, "If we owe the gospel to a converted rabbi, we must suppose that he was not working entirely alone, but that he took an active part in the life of the church where he lived and served. This is tantamount to saying that there was a school at work in the church of Matthew."[4] He sees a continuation of the school of Jesus which goes via the teaching of the apostles and ministers of the word to the school of Matthew. This school served the purpose of training teachers and church leaders. The textbook used in that school happened to be the Gospel of Matthew.

The studies of Kilpatrick and Stendahl are not without merit, yet they do little to answer the question whether Matthew, as Papias indicates, compiled a Gospel in the "Hebrew" language. Roman Catholic scholars have contended that behind the canonical Gospel of Matthew lies a document written by Matthew in the Aramaic dialect. In other words, they claim that Papias was speaking about some kind of a first edition of Matthew's Gospel and that the canonical Gospel of Matthew

---

[2]*Ibid.*, III, 39, 15. Also see C. Steward Petrie, "The Authorship of 'The Gospel According to Matthew'; a Reconsideration of the External Evidence." *New Testament Studies* 14 (1, 1967); p. 31.

[3]*The Origins of the Gospel According to Matthew.* Oxford: Clarendon, 1946; p. 100.

[4]*The School of St. Matthew.* Lund: Gleerup, Copenhagen: Munksgaard, 1954; p. 30.

is a revised edition.[5] Of course, this claim immediately raises further
questions: how was the revised edition composed? Did the author use a
primitive version of the First Gospel and strengthen it by borrowing
from the Gospel of Mark? Did the evangelist actually borrow from
Mark's Gospel? These are some of the questions asked by New
Testament scholars today.

Trying to show that the evangelist reveals his identity somewhat indirectly in the Gospel of Matthew, Edgar J. Goodspeed links the former
tax collector to the First Gospel.[6] He does this by looking at the many
incidents which relate to money: there is the account of Peter paying
the Temple tax for Jesus and himself, by catching a fish with a coin in
its mouth (17:24-27); Jesus tells the parable of the unforgiving servant
who owed his master millions of dollars (18:21-35); and Matthew
includes the parable of the three servants who received from their
master five thousand, two thousand, and one thousand dollars respectively (25:14-30). The first two accounts are found only in Matthew's
Gospel, and the third differs from Luke's parable of the coins in that
the amount of money given to the servants differs greatly. Only a person
who was accustomed to deal with great sums of money could have
written these parables. And the incident of the paying of the Temple
tax took place in Capernaum, where Jesus at one time called Matthew
away from the tollbooth.

Departing from the trend set by form criticism, which considered the
writer of the First Gospel an anonymous collector of individual stories,
the redaction critic views the evangelist as an individual writer. Matthew
is not merely a collector and hander-on of the tradition which he
has received: he also interprets it.[7] The redaction critic, therefore, is
interested in the theology of the Gospel writer.

In an interesting study on the Gospel of Matthew, Ralph P. Martin
analyzes the method employed by the redaction critic in these words:
"The upshot of this new method of gospel study, as applied to the
First Gospel, is to re-instate Matthew as a distinct personality in his
own right and as a church theologian whose recounting of the story of
Jesus tells us more about what Matthew's church thought concerning
the risen Lord than about Jesus' personality and words as these affected
His Galilean audiences."[8]

The redaction critic, Günther Bornkamm, does not mean to imply
that he wants to find the apostolic source for the Gospel in the former
tax collector. There is still a degree of anonymity about the author;

[5]B. C. Butler, *The Originality of St. Matthew.* Cambridge: University Press, 1951.
[6]*Matthew, Apostle and Evangelist.* Philadelphia: Winston, 1959.
[7]G. Bornkamm, G. Barth, H. J. Held, *op. cit.*
[8]"St. Matthew in Recent Study." *Expository Times* 80 (5, 1969); p. 133.

"Matthew" appears in his Gospel, certainly first of all, as the representative of a congregation.[9] Bornkamm is not interested in hunting for names and biographical references. Matthew for him is merely a scribe.

Even though we are interested in the new methods introduced by the redaction critics and appreciate their efforts to show the individual evangelist behind the Synoptic Gospels, we do not think that the testimony of the Church Fathers concerning the Apostle Matthew can be disregarded. The popular idea that the apostle had a hand in writing the Gospel of Matthew is not quite obsolete; in fact, it merits serious consideration.

Characteristics

A characteristic which catches the attention of the observant student of the Gospel of Matthew is the abundance of Old Testament citations. Of course, the author uses these quotations to establish a bridge between the Old Testament Scriptures and the gospel of Jesus: he shows the fulfillment of the Messianic prophecies in the coming of Jesus Christ. However, the question which emerges is whether Matthew relies on the Gospel of Mark at all when he introduces these Old Testament quotations. Robert H. Gundry has made a comprehensive study of these quotations. By comparing the citations from the Old Testament in the Gospels of Matthew, Mark, and Luke, he concludes that the Gospel writers relied on a common tradition. This common tradition consists of a mixed text reflecting the three languages spoken during first-century Palestine: Aramaic, Greek, and Hebrew. Gundry makes this observation: "That this mixed text character pervades all three gospels — not just Q material or Matthean material Lk might have copied from Mt, for Marcan allusive quotations are included — suggests a common body of tradition behind *all three* synoptic gospels."[10]

On the basis of this observation, Gundry ventures the hypothesis that the Apostle Matthew stands behind this common tradition. That is, Matthew, while following Jesus, served as a scribe who took notes. The sayings of Jesus were recorded in a notebook which became the common property of the apostles. According to Gundry, Matthew as an expublican was well trained for such a function. As a tax collector he was accustomed to record all kinds of information; most likely he did so in shorthand. Moreover, Matthew was able to speak the three languages current in Palestine; he was familiar with Old Testament Scriptures in Hebrew, Greek, and Aramaic (targums). Matthew recorded his information rather loosely and informally and made his notes available to Mark and Luke. Consequently, they followed the same outline of

---

[9] *Op. cit.*, p. 49.
[10] *The Use of the Old Testament in St. Matthew's Gospel.* Leiden: Brill, 1967; p. 180.

Jesus' words and works. Gundry concludes by saying, "If then we accept as a working hypothesis that the Apostle Mt stands behind the mixed text elsewhere, it is natural to think the same concerning the formula-citations and the first gospel itself. There is thus no advantage in thinking that the name 'Mt' was erroneously attached to the first gospel because that apostle stood behind an earlier tradition incorporated into the gospel. The distinctive mixed text may betray his presence behind both."[11]

A study of this nature has been most helpful in gaining a better understanding of the common tradition which lies back of the three synoptic Gospels. But to suggest the hypothesis that the Apostle Matthew was first in writing a Gospel account does not answer the question why the writer of Matthew's Gospel seems to depend on the Gospel of Mark. If the Apostle Matthew is standing behind the common tradition of a mixed text, does that also suggest that he wrote the First Gospel as we have it today? That is the question.

Ernest L. Abel argues that the material composed by Matthew and the additional material (the so-called interpolations) is "so excessive and contradictory as to presume that it represents the combined effort of two separate individuals, working independently of one another, and each writing with a different purpose and audience in mind."[12] Thus Abel sees two writers in the First Gospel: one a Jewish-Christian who wrote between A.D. 64 and 70 before the destruction of the temple, and the other a Gentile who composed the Greek edition of Matthew's Gospel in Antioch between A.D. 80 and 105. The weakness of this study is its reliance on hypotheses. For instance, Abel believes that Matthew outlived Peter and Paul only by a few years. He puts the death of Peter and Paul at A.D. 62, and Matthew who did not survive the flight from Jerusalem to Pella during the Roman siege may have died between A.D. 62 and 66. Before that, the apostle wrote his Gospel, which Abel considers to be equivalent to the source Q. This source, which is a compilation of sayings, was written in Jerusalem by Matthew.

However, an original apostolic Gospel must have circulated in the early church, which was more extensive than some undefined composition of sayings called Q. How would the external evidence concerning the existence of a Hebrew (Aramaic) Gospel of Matthew have arisen if there were no truth to it? Besides, if there had been doubt about the apostolic authorship of Matthew's Gospel, the heretics quoting this Gospel would have used this as evidence against the church.

The Gospel of Matthew reveals its own character, its own content, its

---

[11]*Ibid.*, p. 184.
[12]"Who Wrote Matthew?" *New Testament Studies* 17 (2, 1971); p. 138.

own purpose. The name of the apostle has been associated with the First Gospel from the time of the early church. And though many problems remain which cannot be solved except by means of some hypothesis, the Gospel itself exhibits so many traces of its own trend and purpose that it would not be unreasonable to see the hand of the Apostle Matthew.

Summary Statements

The trend fostered by redaction criticism is that of seeing the evangelist as a theologian in his own right. By means of a number of valuable studies, redaction critics have demonstrated the point that Matthew interpreted the gospel tradition he received theologically. Naturally in their studies they stress the element of redaction and tend to pass over the element of tradition. But these elements should be studied in their proper settings: Matthew like the other evangelist does present a theological interpretation of his gospel, but he does not demonstrate a theology of, let us say Paul or the writer to the Hebrews. These two wrote epistles, whereas Matthew a Gospel. And behind Matthew's Gospel stood a gospel tradition of the early church, which was rooted in history. The author of the First Gospel remained true to the historical basis of the tradition and did not surrender it in the interest of his theology. His theology, because of this historical basis underlying the tradition, is therefore established deeply in history. When Matthew writes the words "His blood be on us and on our children" (27:25), he records what the Jewish people shouted in chorus to Pontius Pilate. This is history and not an editorial note of a Gentile redactor who wished to place a curse upon the Jewish people.

Admittedly, the Gospel of Matthew is a gospel of the church. It not only mentions the word "church" twice, but it could also serve as a document for use by the church. Again, the redaction critics have stressed this characteristic in their individual studies. Yet a close examination of the relationship between church and synagogue as reflected in the Gospel of Matthew has become mandatory. Did Matthew write his Gospel for the benefit of the Jewish-Christian community, or was his Gospel meant to be used universally? Douglas R. A. Hare, in a study on the Jewish persecution of Christians, demonstrates that at the time Matthew wrote his Gospel enmity between Christians and the Jewish community had been reduced. "There was little inclination on the part of the Jews to persecute Gentile Christians or to instigate Gentile persecution of the Church. While Christian 'agitators' were occasionally turned over to Gentile authorities for punishment, this kind of persecution is of little concern to Matthew. We may regard it as a rather exceptional procedure and one that for Matthew belongs largely to the past."[13] Matthew seems to indicate that at the time he wrote the Gospel the Jewish synagogue and the Christian church were two distinct institutions: the synagogue he regards as the place where the hypocrites gather.

However, the relation between the Jewish-Christian community and the Gentiles, who had become Christian, should be explored further in the light of the theme of universalism so evident in the First Gospel. In Acts 6, the conflict between the Jewish-Christian and the Greek-speaking Christians comes to light. In the city of Jerusalem, therefore, the church must have consisted of a number of congregations, some Jewish-Christian, others Gentile Christian. If the Gospel of Matthew — because of its many Jewish features such as the numerous Old Testament citations, the constant use of the phrase "kingdom of heaven" in order to avoid using the name "God" as in "kingdom of God," and unexplained Jewish customs — is a Gospel written for the Jews, did Matthew also minister to the needs of the Gentile-Christians in view of his universalistic teaching? The redaction critics studying the Gospel of Matthew will serve their purpose best by coming to a common understanding how the evangelist responds to the needs of the Jewish-Hellenistic church.

In conclusion we wish to refer once again to the two emphases found in the First Gospel: tradition and theology.

Though the redaction critic has devoted his attention to the theology of Matthew and has said little about the gospel tradition which the evangelist received, sooner or later he must face the question concerning the origin of this tradition. Should he say that the evangelist used the Gospel of Mark as a source, he would have to explain how Matthew adopted Mark's text but not his theology. And if the three Synoptic evangelists have received a common tradition, which brought about interdependence among the evangelists, would they have been able to present three separate theologies? In short, the question arises: what, if any, is the relationship between the theology of Matthew, of Mark, and of Luke?

II. MARK

The Gospel that bears the name of Mark is a short story, full of action, relating something of the ministry of Jesus, describing rather fully the suffering and death of Jesus, and having a very brief account of the resurrection. That is the Gospel of Mark.

Because of its brevity, the Second Gospel has not received the atten-

---

[13]*The Theme of Jewish Persecution of Christians in the Gospel According to St. Matthew.* Cambridge: University Press, 1967; p. 169.

tion which the Gospel of Matthew and the Gospel of Luke have enjoyed. Augustine, for example, called Mark "an attendant and abbreviator" of Matthew. Mark had merely condensed the twenty-eight chapters of Matthew to sixteen, so to speak. Until the nineteenth century, this view still prevailed and was advanced by some scholars of the Tübingen school in Germany. The theory, however, did not become influential because the attention of New Testament scholars at that time already was drawn to the structure and the formation of the Second Gospel.

In 1835, Carl Lachmann suggested that Mark, instead of being an abbreviated form of Matthew, was actually the source from which Matthew and Luke had borrowed. This marked the beginning of the period in which the theory of the so-called Marcan priority for many has become an assured result. For them, the Gospel of Mark is one of the main sources from which Matthew and Luke have drawn their material; therefore, Mark is not merely the earliest of the three Synoptics but is the most important.

Composition

"One of the greatest achievements of New Testament criticism in the last century has been to establish beyond reasonable doubt that the Gospel of Mark formed one of the principal sources used both by Matthew and Luke, and that it is both the earliest and in some ways the most important of our gospels."[14]

This comment was made by Richard Heard in 1950 and the majority of New Testament scholars agree. Archibald M. Hunter, who has been called the prince of popularizers, put the whole matter in rhyme.

> The problem solved is stated here:
> Our Mark did first of all appear.
> For Luke and Matthew used him both.
> But Luke and Matthew nothing loth
> to add some more, used Q (for Quelle)
> and each a special source as well.[15]

The certainty for holding forth the banner of Mark's priority is simply rooted in a comparison of the parallel accounts of the three Synoptic Gospels. Merely looking at the order of events which are presented in the Synoptics, scholars point out that Mark either agrees with Matthew or Luke and that quite often all three agree. This fact in itself already is quite meaningful because Mark takes on priority over Matthew and Luke. And this fact is strengthened by the observation that when

---

[14]R. Heard, *An Introduction to the New Testament.* New York: Harper & Row, 1950; p. 53.
[15]*Introducing the New Testament.* London: SCM, 1961; p. 38.

Matthew and Luke agree, they never do so in opposition to Mark. That is, when Matthew and Luke are in agreement, they are in unison with the order of Mark. And that proves the point that Mark is the source for Matthew and Luke.

But that last point can never be presented as an absolute fact. Numerous instances can be shown where Matthew and Luke together depart from the order of events as given by Mark. Scholars from the beginning of the twentieth century until the present have challenged the Marcan priòrity because of the agreement of Matthew and Luke against Mark.[16] Furthermore, they note that if Luke had the Gospel of Mark in front of him when he composed the Third Gospel, why did he omit a rather sizeable section of the ministry of Jesus recorded in Mark 6:45–8:26? This section covers nearly two chapters in that part of the Gospel of Mark which deals with the ministry of Jesus. What some scholars are trying to say is this: though it is rather easy to assert that the Gospel of Mark was used as a source by both Matthew and Luke, when all the available facts are considered much of the certainty has been weakened.

Nevertheless, the majority of scholars are of the opinion that the Gospel of Mark is still first among the Synoptics. They feel that the theory of Marcan priority still solves more problems and answers more questions than any other theory. Matthew and Luke depend for their information on Mark and on the hypothetical source called Q. With the aid of a few lines, we get the following scheme:

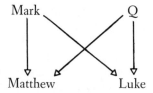

This scheme is known as the "two-document theory." Matthew and Luke make use of two sources, namely Mark and Q. Some scholars have added to this number of sources two others: M (for a source used by Matthew) and L (a source used by Luke). Though this graphic scheme has gained common acceptance, difficulties remain. For example, what happened to the oral gospel which Jesus taught and which the apostles stabilized in the period between the outpouring of the Holy

[16]See e.g. E. A. Abbott, *Correction of Mark*. London, 1901. W. R. Farmer, *The Synoptic Problem*. D. L. Dungan, "Mark–The Abridgement of Matthew and Luke." *Perspective* 11 (1-2, 1970); pp. 51-97.

Spirit and the writing of the canonical Gospels? Moreover, to say something meaningful about a source called Q with no written proof for its existence as such is quite difficult. And last, what sources did Mark use for the composition of his Gospel? Because if Mark relied on a reference (oral tradition or an informant) could not Matthew and Luke have done the same, especially since Luke indicates as much in the introduction to the Third Gospel?

Sources and Author

Would we know who the author of the Second Gospel is if we should remove the superscription: The Gospel according to Mark? This superscription, in fact, was not added to the Gospel until about A.D. 125. Authors in the ancient world rather modestly might attach their name to the end of the manuscript. Granted for the sake of the argument that Mark added his name to the bottom of his manuscript and that the last page, so to speak, was lost soon after it was written, the readers would not know who composed this Gospel. Tradition, however, unanimously ascribes this document to Mark, the follower of Peter.

According to Acts, Mark had a first name, John. His mother must have been a well-to-do lady living in a spacious house in Jerusalem, who opened her doors to apostles and early Christians (12:12). John Mark spent his youth in Jerusalem and in later years lived in Antioch where he, together with his cousin Barnabas, accompanied Paul on his first missionary journey to Cyprus (13:5). Despite the initial separation which arose between Paul on the one side and John Mark on the other (15:37ff.), the differences must have been dissolved and John Mark together with Barnabas became Paul's faithful followers. In his letter to the Colossians, for example, Paul sends greetings from Mark (4:10). And at the end of Paul's life while awaiting the death sentence, Paul writes to Timothy, "Get Mark and bring him with you; for he is very useful in serving me" (II Tim. 4:11). Mark must have been known to the church at Colossae, for his name is also mentioned in Paul's letter to Philemon (v. 24) who lived in that town. Paul himself had not founded the church there, but may have preached the gospel to the Colossians. What is more to the point is Paul's description of Mark. He calls him his fellow worker. That is, Mark worked together with Paul in the proclamation of the gospel; the apostle's teaching was transmitted by Mark so that he became part in the chain of receiving and delivering a tradition.

How much John Mark may have heard from Jesus cannot be verified. The reference to the young man in the Garden of Gethsemane, who was going to be arrested, lost his linen shirt, and fled naked, may or may not refer to John Mark (Mark 14:51f.). What we do detect, however, is an intimate knowledge of the city of Jerusalem on the part of the writer of the Second Gospel. To mention one example, Mark's reference to the court of the high priest's residence is much more precise than that of the other evangelists. Mark writes, "And as Peter was *below* in the courtyard" (14:66). Matthew at this point says that Peter was sitting *outside* in the courtyard (Matt. 26:69) and Luke and John omit this descriptive detail. The difference between the words *below* and *outside* is significant, because it indicates that Mark was not only acquainted with the layout but knew the very construction of the courtyard: there were two levels. The courtyard was on a lower level than the court room where Jesus was questioned. Mark was familiar with the location. Whether Mark himself was present remains an open question.

Besides being in Paul's company for many years, Mark also followed Peter. At the end of his first epistle, Peter sends greeting of Mark and affectionately calls him "my son" (5:13). Of course, this refers to a spiritual father-son relationship. Peter had come to love Mark as his own son because of their work in the gospel ministry.

The New Testament has no more to say about John Mark, but the Church Fathers do. Eusebius, the church historian, records the well-known remark of Papias:

> And the Presbyter [the Apostle John] used to say this, "Mark became Peter's interpreter and wrote accurately all that he remembered, not, indeed, in order, of the things said or done by the Lord, nor had he followed him, but later on, as I said, followed Peter, who used to give teaching as necessity demanded but not making, as it were, an arrangement of the Lord's oracles, so that Mark did nothing wrong in thus writing down single points as he remembered them. For to one thing he gave attention, to leave out nothing of what he had heard and to make no false statements in them."[17]

The other Church Fathers virtually say the same thing. Therefore, the evidence coming by way of tradition is very strong. Mark wrote the Second Gospel. We may add that as his informants Peter and Paul take an honorable place.

That Mark wrote the gospel of Jesus Christ and not the gospel of Peter is evident from the first line of his Gospel account: "The beginning of the gospel of Jesus Christ, the Son of God." In how far the author relied on the instruction of Peter has been a point of much debate. Even though he received source material from Peter, he remained an author in his own right. Did Mark have access to other material, written or oral? Robin S. Barbour queries, "Also important are the questions whether Mark knew Q (if indeed Q was a written

---

[17]Eusebius, *Ecclesiastical History* (III, 39, 15).

source), and whether other written sources known to him can be isolated. There would be widespread agreement that the Passion narrative had been committed to writing in some form before Mark, but attempts to identify other written sources behind Mark have not on the whole carried conviction."[18]

Interpretation

Mark is the writer of the Second Gospel.

This remark sounds somewhat simplistic, self-evident, and matter-of-fact. For decades however, the form critic has regarded the author of Mark's Gospel as an anonymous collector of individual stories about Jesus; the collector put these stories together in such a way that they formed a continuous narrative. The connective links which he inserted can easily be detected; for instance, in introducing two stories about sabbath observance, he inserts the remark "One sabbath he was going through the grainfields" (2:23) for the one story and "Again he entered the synagogue" (3:1) for the other. These insertions are called editorial embellishments by the form critic; they contribute nothing to the story itself.

For the form critic, the evangelists remained anonymous. And the Synoptics could just as well be labelled: Gospel I, Gospel II, and Gospel III. Designating them as the First, Second and Third Gospel respectively, indicates that the writing of the documents is of little consequence: the evangelist merely collected existing stories and put them — by inserting connecting links — in a somewhat continuous order.

But why did the individual evangelist put the stories in the order he chose? Since he does not always portray a chronological sequence of events, what was the purpose, the motif of the writer? These are the questions asked by the redaction critics.

The redaction critic has put the first three Gospels in parallel columns. He notices that each evangelist has a different approach in the writing of his Gospel. The individual evangelist expresses a religious concern, which distinguishes him from the other writers of the gospel. The evangelist, in other words, is a person with a purpose.

The redaction critic has reinstated the evangelist as a writer. And by comparing the parallel gospel accounts, he has pointed out that the evangelist works as an individual theologian. He received the gospel tradition which he in his own writing interpreted theologically. "Each evangelist is not only a tradent [a person who hands down a tradition],

---

[18]"Recent Study of the Gospel According to St. Mark." *Expository Times* 79 (11, 1968), p. 325.

but, above all, reworks from a theological point of view the material which he passes on."[19]

The form critic presents the Gospel writer as a person who worked with scissors and paste, piecing together the stories about Jesus. The redaction critic, on the other hand, recognizes the personality of the individual evangelist by calling him a theologian in his own right. "The aim of Redaction criticism is to place the gospel in the setting of the evangelist's situation, or of the situation of the Christian community of which he was a member."[20]

It was Willi Marxsen, who in 1956 asked the question why Mark wrote his Gospel. There must have been some reason why the evangelist composed his Gospel. According to Marxsen, the reason lies in the historical situation of the years before the destruction of Jerusalem in A.D. 70. In those years, Mark wrote his Gospel to warn the Christians of the impending catastrophe, to advise them to flee to Galilee, and to remind them that Jesus would appear to them there (Mark 16:7).[21] Wherefore, Mark wrote his Gospel to tell the church that Jesus would appear to the believers in Galilee. And with that information, in the opinion of Marxsen, the evangelist ended his account.

A number of facts militate against this theory set forth by the redaction critic. For one thing, when the angel told the women that they must instruct the disciples and Peter to go to Galilee where they would see Jesus, he did not imply that they would have to wait more than thirty-five years for this event. The Gospel of Matthew, in fact, provides the information that the disciples listened to the instruction given them by the women. "Now the eleven disciples went to Galilee to the mountain to which Jesus had directed them. And when they saw him, they worshipped him" (28:16, 17).

Next, tradition puts the composition of the Second Gospel in Rome; it was written at the request of the Gentile Christians there. Clement of Alexandria transmits an ancient tradition concerning the place and purpose of composition. Says he,

> When Peter had publicly preached the word at Rome, and by the Spirit had proclaimed the Gospel, that those present, who were many, exhorted Mark, as one who had followed him for a long time and remembered what had been spoken, to make a record of what was said; and that he did this, and distributed the Gospel among those that asked him. And that when the matter came to Peter's knowledge he neither strongly forbade it nor urged it forward.[22]

---

[19]H.-D. Knigge, "The Meaning of Mark." *Interpretation* 22 (1, 1968), p. 54.
[20]R. P. Martin, "The Life-setting of Mark." *Expository Times* 80 (12, 1969), p. 362.
[21]*Op. cit.*
[22]Eusebius, *op. cit.* (VI, 14, 6 and II, 15, 1-2).

That the Gospel was written for Gentile Christians and not for the Palestinian church is evident throughout. The evangelist explains Jewish customs, translates Aramaic words, uses many Latin words, and in general addresses the Gospel to the Gentile reader.

Last, why should Mark have written a Gospel for the Christians in Jerusalem, warning them to flee to Galilee and informing them that there they would see Jesus as he promised, if Jesus would personally appear in Galilee? If the return of Jesus were so imminent that the believers would see him in Galilee, the need for writing a Gospel would have disappeared.

Using the popular version *Good News for Modern Man* as his basic English text, Eduard Schweizer has written a commentary on the Gospel of Mark. He follows in the footsteps of Marxsen by stressing the theology of Mark. However, when it concerns matters of source history, author, and geography, the commentator deviates from traditional theology. The sources for the Gospel itself are to be found somewhere in a community of Syria; and in respect to the author of the Gospel, Schweizer refuses to acknowledge John Mark. He wants to follow the redaction critical method, and wants to see the hand of the theologian in the Second Gospel. Yet when it comes to identifying Mark of the New Testament with the author of Mark's Gospel, Schweizer demurs. For him, Mark is not the author of the Second Gospel.[23]

Tradition itself indicates that the purpose of Mark's Gospel is theological, though not without a historical basis. When the redaction critic stresses this theological purpose rather than the historical, he is correct, because Mark was not interested in writing a complete biography of Jesus. But when the redaction critic places historical incidents and geographical concepts on the altar of theology, he is offering a strange sacrifice. Certainly Mark's theological purpose is important, but this concern does not give the redaction critic the liberty to relegate history and geography to the realm of theological symbols.

In the opinion of Marxsen, historical events connected with the ministry of Jesus are unimportant because they are subordinate to Mark's theological motif. For this reason, Marxsen displays a conscious effort to de-historicize the Second Gospel in the interest of tracing the theological purpose of the evangelist. Granted that historical facts may have theological significance, we cannot sever their relation to the historical event. In order to assume theological significance, these facts must relate to actual events. And this is supported by the testimony of the early Church Fathers, who mention that Mark wrote accurately the things said and done by the Lord.

---

[23]*The Good News According to Mark*. Richmond: Knox, 1970.

III. LUKE

The introductions to the Third Gospel and the book of Acts have this in common that both refer to a certain Theophilus. In fact, both writings are dedicated to this person. The first five verses of Acts, moreover, link this book to the Gospel of Luke, so that this summary is somewhat of a bridge. "This summary has the form that is usual in classical literature whenever a book consists of more than one volume. It appears, therefore, that the gospel and the Acts together formed one work which was, for technical reasons, published in two volumes."[24] For this reason, we look at the Third Gospel as well as the Acts.

Author

Paul calls Luke "the beloved physician" (Col. 4:14). As Paul's traveling companion Luke does record medical cases with great precision, for example, the snake bite of Paul on Malta and the healing of Publius, chief of that island, "sick with fever and dysentery" (Acts 28:1-10). Throughout the Gospel and the Acts, Luke makes use of a medical vocabulary, so that Paul's expression "beloved physician" is not at all out of place.

When W. K. Hobart wrote *The Medical Language of St. Luke* in 1882, claiming that the evangelist was a physician, he remained unchallenged for many decades. That is, until 1920. In that year H. J. Cadbury published a monograph entitled *The Style and Literary Method of Luke,* in which he critically examined the medical terms used in the Third Gospel and Acts. He came to the conclusion that these terms are not peculiar to Luke; they also occur in the writings of Plutarch, Lucian, Josephus, and in the Septuagint. Cadbury doubted the validity of Hobart's thesis. "By the same token our evangelist could be made a lawyer as well as a doctor on the basis of many legal terms which he uses, especially in the closing chapters of Acts, while in the story of the shipwreck, if we are to believe Wellhausen, the doctor and lawyer are metamorphosed into an expert mariner."[25]

As a result, Cadbury maintained that the medical language in the Gospel of Luke and the Acts does not prove that the writer was a physician. And in this respect, he is correct. However, this argument cannot be used to discredit Lucan authorship, for the simple reason that Cadbury's arguments do not say anything against Lucan authorship. Nor can this study be used to say that Luke could not have been a physician. The medical terms found in Luke's Gospel and the Acts, in fact, strengthen the tradition that Luke the physician wrote these books.

---

[24] A. F. J. Klijn, *An Introduction to the New Testament.* Leiden: Brill, 1967; p. 36.
[25] *The Making of Luke-Acts.* London: S.P.C.K., 1961; p. 220.

The point is that Cadbury's investigation cannot be used to disprove that Luke wrote the Gospel and Acts.

The writer of Luke's Gospel and the Acts intended his work to be a unit. Undoubtedly, because of its content, the early Christian church put the Gospel with those of Matthew and Mark. Thus, the Third Gospel was read and studied in the context of the Synoptics. Lately, however, the two documents of Luke are usually combined in any kind of study which treats the historicity of the accounts. When a study is made of the historical accuracy of recorded incidents in the writings of Luke, both works have to be consulted. The writings of Luke must be placed within a historical and geographical framework because, as a historian, Luke is intent on recording an accurate and trustworthy account of the life of Jesus and the ministry of the apostles. He puts his writings in the context of world history: Jesus was born during the reign of Caesar Augustus at the time when Quirinius was governor of Syria; John the Baptist came to the Jordan in the fifteenth year of the reign of Tiberius Caesar when Pontius Pilate was governor of Judea; and Paul came to the island of Cyprus when Sergius Paulus was in charge as proconsul.

In regard to Luke's documents, scholars may approach the question of historicity either positively or negatively. Positively, they take Luke's account at face value until he is proven wrong. Negatively, they are unwilling to accept Luke's narrative as historically correct until he is proven right. I. Howard Marshall offers this sage advice: "There is good reason to approach (Luke's) Gospel with the assumption that sound history may be found in it than to begin by pronouncing a negative verdict against him."[26] A plea, in brief, for a positive approach!

Luke the Historian

Is Luke really the historian among writers of the New Testament? Are his two volumes really historical works? May we call the Acts the history book of the early Christian church? These and other questions are frequently asked by modern scholars. They point out that Luke is not at all complete in presenting his material, that he shows no precision in providing historical details, and that even a chronology is lacking in the Gospel and in Acts.

Other writers take Luke at his word. They point to the introduction of the Third Gospel, where the author states that he examined all things closely, "that you may know the *truth* concerning the things of which you have been informed, most excellent Theophilus" (1:4). It is clear

---

[26]"Recent Study of the Gospel According to St. Luke." *Expository Times* 80 (1, 1968), p. 7. Also see his *Luke: Historian and Theologian*. p. 75.

from the introduction that Luke has spared time nor effort to report accurately what took place. Also in describing the events as recorded in Acts, for instance, the trial of Paul in Jerusalem and Caesarea, the writer gives an accurate account with the necessary details for the background of the narrative. If Luke has taken the effort to be accurate in reporting the more extensive narratives, one may expect that Luke has shown that same dedication to the truth in reporting accounts which are less detailed. "According to his own testimony Luke wished to be taken seriously as a historian."[27] In harmony with literary criteria, the reader should grant him this wish.

In the Gospel, Luke is rather explicit in his sketch of the political situation of Palestine. After his introduction, he mentions the name of Herod, king of Judea. In Chapter 2, he places Judea in the broader context of the Roman Empire by referring to the decree of Caesar Augustus at whose command Quirinius conducted a census. The third chapter is still more explicit: Luke sketches the political and religious situation by stating that John the Baptist received the word of the Lord during the fifteenth year of the reign of Tiberius Caesar, while Pontius Pilate was governor of Judea, Herod tetrarch of Galilee, his brother Philip tetrarch of Iturea and Trachonitis, Lysanias tetrarch of Abilene, and Annas and Caiaphas were high priests. Throughout the Gospel Luke calls attention to Herod the tetrarch; especially at the end of the Gospel that name is prominent.

In the book of Acts, however, Luke does not provide too many details about the political situation in Palestine. In Chapter 12, a certain King Herod is putting the Apostle James to death and imprisons Peter. Roman governors are mentioned, in Chapters 23 and following, by the names of Felix and Festus. And finally, in Chapter 25, Luke introduces a certain King Agrippa. In the broader framework of the Roman Empire, the name of Claudius appears twice.

Is Luke an accurate historian, for it appears that the references to political figures are rather confusing? If Felix and Festus were governors of Judea and Galilee, how could Agrippa be king over that same region?

We learn from the Jewish historian, Flavius Josephus, that the historical references, given in Acts, are accurate and pertinent. Though Luke at first sight may give the reader a bewildering array of names, titles, and places, within the context of the middle of the first century Luke's narrative is trustworthy and authentic. Because of the unrest among the Jewish people, the Roman government had to change its policies regarding the rule of Palestine from time to time. After the

---

[27]Marshall, *Luke,* p. 41.

death of Herod the Great in 4 B.C., Judea was governed by his son Archelaus (Matt. 2:22) and Galilee by another son, called Herod Antipas. Whereas Herod Antipas ruled Galilee for many decades, from 4 B.C., to A.D. 39, his brother Archelaus was removed from office within a decade and replaced by governors directly appointed by the Roman Emperor. Hence, Pontius Pilate ruled Judea during the reign of Herod Antipas in Galilee.

Herod Antipas was deposed in A.D. 39 and was replaced by his nephew, Herod Agrippa I. Emperor Claudius was kindly disposed to him and enlarged his territory by giving him the territories of Judea and Samaria. Thus the Jerusalem church was persecuted by King Herod Agrippa, who killed James, the brother of John, and imprisoned Peter (Acts 12:2, 3). He wanted to gain the favor of the Jews, who had become increasingly hostile to the Roman government. Herod Agrippa I ruled only a few years. An angel of the Lord, says Luke in Acts 12:23, smote him, so that he died a sudden and unexpected death. Josephus, in his *Antiquities* (19.8.2), attests to the accuracy of the report by describing the same event, though in greater detail.

The successor to Herod Agrippa I was his sixteen or seventeen-year son, Agrippa. Despite his youthful age, Emperor Claudius did appoint him to succeed his father. However, he was not given the territories of Judea, Samaria, and Galilee because they proved to be too troublesome. Instead, Roman governors were appointed to rule these areas, of whom Felix and Festus are known to us because of Paul's imprisonment in Caesarea. Felix is mentioned in Acts 23:24ff.; he was replaced, while Paul was in prison, by Festus. While Festus was in office, he was visited by Agrippa, the son of Herod Agrippa I. This son, who called himself King Herod Agrippa II, was given a kingdom which extended to the northeast of the Galilean lake. He lived in the capital city of Caesarea Philippi. When governor Festus assumed office in A.D. 59, King Agrippa traveled from Caesarea Philippi to Caesarea to welcome him (Acts 25:13). It was during this visit that he listened to Paul preaching and exclaimed: "In a short time you think to make me a Christian!"[28]

Luke's credentials as a historian are time-tested and valid. It would appear utterly unfair to discredit the historical accuracy of this writer. Even though Luke's historical details may be somewhat scanty, he must be considered a reliable historian.

The discussion, however, does not center on the historicity of these works but rather on the purpose of writing. The question which has

---

28G. E. Ladd, *The Young Church: Acts of the Apostles,* London: Butterworth, and New York and Nashville: Abingdon, 1964, p. 14ff. Also see, I. H. Marshall, "Recent Study of the Acts of the Apostles" *Expository Times* 80 (10, 1969), pp. 292-296.

been the center of discussion for some time is whether Luke's purpose in writing the Gospel and Acts has been prompted by the author's theological interests. That is, the question of the character and purpose of the Third Gospel and Acts has been approached from a redaction-critical stance.

Purpose

What does the redaction critic say about the literary productions of Luke? For one thing, he does not regard the writer as a historian but as a theologian. And as a theologian, "Luke is in no way motivated by a desire to exercise historical accuracy, but entirely by his theological concept of the role" which names and places assume in the history of salvation.[29]

The German New Testament scholar, Hans Conzelmann, has been first in emphasizing the theological interests of Luke to the extent that the entire concept of historicity has been changed. Events, names of places, and names of persons in the Third Gospel are considered by Conzelmann from a symbolical point of view because Luke was not interested in presenting an accurate historical account but in establishing his theological aims. Luke, according to Conzelmann, took his material for the Gospel from his sources and edited the material in order to fit his theology. Whereas the source material constantly portrayed the end of time as being near, Luke, looking objectively at the period of history since the death and resurrection of Jesus, came to the conclusion that the period between the resurrection of Jesus and the end of time must be a considerable interval. Hence Conzelmann has divided history in three periods; first, the period of Israel during the time of the Law and the prophets; second, the period of Jesus' ministry on earth; and third, the period between Jesus' ministry and his return. Conzelmann, therefore, concludes that Luke wrote his Gospel about the second period of time, but in writing the content of his Gospel he looked at the third period — the period of the church and the Spirit. Appropriately, Conzelmann has entitled his book on the Third Gospel *Die Mitte der Zeit*, which means "the middle-point of time." In English translation the book appears under the title *The Theology of St. Luke*.[30]

In other words, Luke did not apply the teaching of Jesus concerning the end to the second period of time (the middle-point of time) but to the last period, the period of the church. Luke wanted to postpone the crises of the end time. By contrast, Mark did not do that when he wrote the Second Gospel. In Mark 13, the chapter of Jesus' discourse

---

[29]N. Perrin, *What Is Redaction Criticism?* Philadelphia: Fortress, 1969, p. 29.
[30]*The Theology of St. Luke*. New York: Harper & Row, 1960.

on the last things, wars, rumors of wars, earthquakes and famines are mentioned. Mark put these events in his own context by concluding, "these things are the beginning of sorrows" (v. 8). But, in the parallel passage in Luke, this conclusion is lacking.

Another example can be taken from the Acts of the Apostles. In the second chapter, Luke quotes at length from the prophecy of Joel, which relates the outpouring of the Spirit and the signs and portents of the end of time (vv. 17-21). For Joel the words applied to the end of time, but Luke, who reports the fulfilment of this prophecy in the outpouring of the Holy Spirit, cannot say that the end of time has come. Instead he must indicate that the coming of the Holy Spirit is the beginning of the end of time. The outpouring of the Spirit ushered in the last period of time, namely that of the church.

What Luke, in the opinion of Conzelmann, has done is to place the teachings of the end of time not in the context of Jesus' ministry; rather, Luke put the doctrine of the last things in the context of the last period of time, the period of the church. The early Christians were wrong in thinking that the end of time was near because they were living in the last days. Luke dispels that thinking by teaching the postponement of the immediate signs and the portents of the end of time. He is interested in the time of the church during which the gospel is preached to all nations.

While Conzelmann concentrated on the Third Gospel, his New Testament colleague Ernst Haenchen looked at the book of Acts by writing a massive volume in the Meyer commentary series and giving it the German title *Apostelgeschichte* (a history of the apostles.)[31] But does Luke really present history as events that really happened, or does he work out his narratives around a theological purpose: the spread of the Word of God and the growth of the church? By reading the account of Acts objectively, we do come to the conclusion that the apostles do not spread the Word of God and do not catch the vision of bringing the gospel to the Gentiles. In fact, because of the death of Stephen and the subsequent persecution of the Christians of Jerusalem, the Word was preached in Judea, Samaria, Phoenicia, Cyprus, and Antioch. The apostles, however, were not persecuted and stayed in Jerusalem. Moreover, not the church of Jerusalem initiated the mission program of evangelizing the Greco-Roman world. The Gentile Christian congregation of Antioch saw "the fields white for the harvest" and commissioned Paul and Barnabas to preach the gospel on the island of Cyprus, throughout Asia Minor, and Greece. The twelve apostles (with the exception of Peter) are never portrayed as preachers of the gospel —

31*Die Apostelgeschichte*. Gottingen: Vandenhoeck & Ruprecht, 1956.

they simply disappear from the scene. Paul is appointed as apostle to the Gentiles, yet Luke does not give his readers personal details concerning Paul, apart from the conversion account (which is reported three times), his three missionary journeys, his arrest, and his voyage and journey to Rome.

History Writing

"What sort of judgment does Luke invite us to pass on his book? If it is to be judged as fundamentally a historical work, whether a continuous narrative or a set of biographical sketches, then the question that must be asked (if we exclude purely artistic issues) is whether Luke gives us the story of events 'as they actually happened.' Does he put the right people in the right places at the right times? Does he represent accurately not only their deeds and words but also their motives and intentions? Does he give the right connections between events?"[32] We really ought to view the two volumes of Luke as one book, and doing this we are able to find answers to the questions just raised.

Luke had to deal with two periods of history, first the time of Jesus' earthly life, and second the origin, growth, and development of the New Testament church. He bridged these two periods by means of the post-resurrection appearances of Jesus and the ascension of Jesus. These accounts are mentioned in the last chapter of his Gospel and then repeated in the first chapter of Acts. The principal person who crosses that bridge from the one period of time to the other is Jesus. "Since the ascension is for Luke both the end of the ministry of Jesus, in which His life finds the triumphant conclusion that gives it meaning, and the beginning of the Church, which makes the life of the Church both possible and intelligible, it follows that, in Luke's thought, the end of the story of Jesus is the Church; and, the story of Jesus is the beginning of the Church. In this proposition lies the distinctive characteristics of Luke's work."[33] Though Luke does not use John's idiom that Jesus is the alpha and the omega, the beginning and the end, he in fact relates the same message.

How did Luke write the book of Acts? In such a way that the book is a continuation of the Gospel. The speeches, for example, all bring the message of Jesus: Peter on the day of Pentecost preached Jesus by relating His life, death, and resurrection; Paul on the Areopagus of Athens brought the news of Jesus' resurrection. By means of the speeches in the book of Acts, Luke shows that the result of the life of Jesus is the rise and development of the church.

---

[32]C. K. Barrett, *Luke the Historian in Recent Study*. Philadelphia: Fortress, pp. 51f.
[33]*Ibid.*, p. 57.

The author of the Third Gospel does not attempt to write a full biographical sketch of Jesus. The gaps in the life of Jesus are too wide despite the birth narrative and the account of the twelve-year-old Jesus in the temple. Luke focuses attention on Jesus, who is the founder of the church. Thus, in the book of Acts, Luke paints the same design. Many gaps in the history of the early church are most obvious; only a few people are predominant so that the book could very well be called "The Acts of Peter and Paul." However, in the book of Acts Luke calls attention to the continuing work of the founder of the church. That is the theme which Luke began in the writing of his Gospel and especially in view of redaction criticism, is whether Luke in his writings continues in the history book of the early church.

The question which has been raised and which is most relevant, especially in view of redaction criticism, is whether Luke in his writings presents himself as an historian or as a theologian. Did Luke intend to write history, guided by the Holy Spirit, to show God's plan and purpose? Or did Luke construct a theology for which he used a historical framework?

Luke as Theologian

That Luke the writer of the Gospel and Acts reveals himself as a theologian cannot be questioned. In that respect, the research on the writings of Luke has not been without profit to the student of the New Testament; he has been introduced to a new dimension of Lucan studies. He sees Luke as a theologian in his own right. However, the very fact that Luke wrote as a theologian may not be used to disregard the fact that Luke also wrote as a historian. Luke did not merely write theological treatises for the benefit of the early church. Luke wrote a historical account of the life of Jesus by tracing accurately everything which had happened (Luke 1:1-4).

The point at issue is whether Luke presents both history and theology or whether he presents sound theology but historical facts may be questionable. In the opinion of Conzelmann, for example, the geography of Luke should not be understood to be historically accurate. Luke does not have an accurate knowledge of the geography of Palestine. Therefore, the geographical references should be understood theologically. Conzelmann even makes geographical locations symbolical, whereby the desert is associated with temptation, the mountain with heavenly communication, the open plain with meeting crowds of people, and the sea with supernatural power. For this reason, he has virtually bypassed the so-called travel section in the Gospel of Luke. He devotes only a few pages to the section 9:51—19:27 because of its reference to Samaria. And because Luke's geographical knowledge of the area is far from correct, so the argument goes, the section must be understood theologically. Says Conzelmann, "The whole country seems to be viewed from abroad. Luke is familiar with the coastal region of Phoenicia, and in Acts with the connection of Judaea with the coast. He appears to think of Galilee as inland, but adjoining Judaea, and of Samaria as being to the north of Judaea."[34]

Certainly Luke was not a Palestinian by birth, but as reported, an Antiochean. Nevertheless, to indicate that a large section of the Gospel was written solely from a theological point of view and that it has no geographical significance is undermining the historical trustworthiness of Luke's report. Luke did have a personal acquaintance with Palestine, which he indicates in the book of Acts. He accompanied Paul on his missionary journey which also brought him to Caesarea, Judea, and Jerusalem.

Luke, however, does not want us to look at his work along narrow historical lines, because his reporting of the facts reveals his theology. In short, Luke is interpreting the facts which he has gathered and he interprets them theologically. No one can fault Luke for this, for if he had merely given the facts of the life of Jesus he would have written a catalogue of events, which would not be a Gospel account. Luke wrote history but looked at the historical account as a theologian who wanted to present Jesus Christ. Therefore, we do not have to ask whether Luke did the right thing in giving his readers interpreted history. Rather, we become aware of the fact that all four evangelists give the readers history interpreted from a theological point of view. As Leon Morris has put it, "There is theology in all of them. It is increasingly accepted in modern writing that all four Gospels are basically theological documents. None is an objectively written piece of history."[35]

Luke wrote his Gospel in order to persuade "the most excellent Theophilus" of the certainty of the things in which he had been instructed. In his introduction to his Gospel he is telling his readers what he is going to do with the information received from the "eyewitnesses and ministers of the word." Luke wrote his Gospel for the many "God-fearing ones" in the Greco-Roman world who had heard from the Jews about the true God. And through the proclamation of the oral gospel they learned about the coming of the Son of God, Jesus Christ.

IV. JOHN

The study of the Gospel according to John has been very rewarding and exciting, especially in view of archaeological and manuscript dis-

---

[34]Op. cit., p. 70.
[35]Studies in the Fourth Gospel. Grand Rapids: Eerdmans, 1969, p. 78.

coveries. By way of introduction to the Johannine studies, let us look at the date of the Fourth Gospel. Tradition puts the date late in the first century. It is Irenaeus, bishop of Lyon during the second century, who makes the following comment: "Afterwards, John, the disciple of the Lord, who also had leaned upon His breast, did himself publish a Gospel during his residence at Ephesus in Asia."[36] Tradition, however, was generally repudiated by many scholars. They placed the date in the middle of the second century because of the fact that the Gospel of John was not known earlier. C. K. Barrett simply concludes: "To trace the influence of the Fourth Gospel upon Christian theology would be more than the task of a lifetime; to trace its influence upon the thought of the first half of the second century is easy, for it had none."[37] But Barrett and all others who have held to a mid-second century date for the Fourth Gospel have had to revise their thinking.

The discovery of the so-called Roberts fragment, a papyrus fragment of the Gospel of John found in the sands of Egypt, changed the thinking of many theologians. This fragment could be dated to a period between A.D. 125 and 140 and presumably closer to the beginning of that period. This means that the Gospel of John already circulated in Egypt around the year A.D. 125. Also, if the Gospel was written in Ephesus, some time must have elapsed before it reached Egypt. Conservatively speaking, at least twenty-five years must be allowed. In other words, the finding of this small papyrus fragment verifies tradition that the Gospel was written toward the end of the first century.

Author

Though the writer of the Fourth Gospel claims to be an eyewitness (19:35; 21:24) and of the four evangelists is the only one who makes this claim, and though internal as well as external evidence points in the direction of apostolic authorship, scholars are not ready to lend support to this view. Leon Morris sums it up in these words: "From all this it is plain that there is still good reason for thinking of the apostle John as the author of the Fourth Gospel. It is far from being a fashionable view. Even among fairly conservative critics many prefer to hold that the apostle was the witness behind the Gospel rather than its actual author. Neither apostolic nor nonapostolic authorship can be held to have been proved up to the hilt."[38] This may seem surprising, yet many writers on Johannine studies simply do not even talk about authorship any more. For them it is settled that John the apostle did not write the Fourth Gospel. Rudolf Bultmann, who wrote a massive commentary

---

[36]*Adv. Haer.* III. i, 1. Grand Rapids: Eerdmans, 1962, p. 414.
[37]*The Gospel According to St. John.* London: S.P.C.K., 1965, p. 52.
[38]*Op. cit.,* p. 264.

on the Gospel of John, simply dismisses evidence that the Apostle John was the author. And the reference to the eyewitness (19:35; 21:24) is, in the opinion of Bultmann, merely a reference added by an ecclesiastical redactor.[39] Yet a number of conservative scholars have examined the evidence available and do hold to apostolic authorship for the Fourth Gospel.

Those scholars who have taken the effort to survey and analyze all the evidence (external and internal) for apostolic authorship attribute the Fourth Gospel to John the apostle. In the latter half of the nineteenth century, B. F. Westcott made a thorough study of all the available evidence[40] and in the middle of the twentieth, Ethelbert Stauffer, among others, has studied the facts. Stauffer comes to this conclusion: "In view of all this we have sufficient ground to ascribe these five writings (i.e., the Fourth Gospel, the three Epistles of John, and Revelation) to a common author of remarkable individuality and great significance, and to identify him as the apostle John."[41]

One of the major objections to Johannine authorship is the difference in style and diction between the first three Gospels and the Fourth Gospel. The Synoptics (Matthew, Mark, and Luke) contain a number of parables spokes by Jesus, John has none. Instead, John has many discourses of Jesus which are so meditative in nature that it is at times difficult to determine where the words of Jesus end and the meditations of John begin. Were the words of John 3:16 "For God so loved the world . . ." spoken by Jesus or is this a meditative reflection of the writer of the Gospel? Because of this objection, many scholars (even conservatives) find it convenient to say that though the Apostle John was influential in teaching the thoughts of the Gospel, one of his followers actually wrote the Fourth Gospel.

Despite the fact that the objection seems formidable, a close look at the entire problem is not only very enlightening but also reassuring. For example, the author of the Fourth Gospel does not repeat the material found in the Synoptic Gospels, except for such incidents as the feeding of the five thousand and the walking of Jesus on the Lake of Galilee. The Fourth Gospel is clearly supplementary to the preceding three. Moreover, the difference in style between the Synoptics and the Gospel of John may be because of a difference in environment. The Synoptics portray Jesus teaching the crowds in Galilee, John reveals that Jesus conversed with Nicodemus, the Pharisee of Jerusalem. A difference in environment and audience brings about a difference in style.

On the other hand, we should not be too rash either in setting the

---

[39]*The Gospel of John.* Philadelphia: Westminster, 1971; pp. 483ff.
[40]*The Gospel According to St. John.* Grand Rapids: Eerdmans, reprint, 1954.
[41]*New Testament Theology.* London: SCM, 1955, p. 41.

Fourth Gospel over against the other three. Much of what is called Johannine style and wording is also found in the other three Gospels. A few examples will illustrate this point. A typical Johannine phrase is "him who sent me." That phrase also occurs in Matthew 10:40, Mark 9:37, and Luke 9:48. And the text found in Matthew 11:27 (and in the parallel passage Luke 10:22) could have been lifted straight out of the Fourth Gospel: "All things have been delivered to me by my Father, and no one knows the Son except the Father, nor does anyone know the Father except the Son and any to whom the Son is willing to reveal him."

What about the meditative aspect of the Fourth Gospel? Jesus, in the tradition of rabbinical teaching of his day, taught his disciples informally as well as formally. Formally he taught his followers parables and sayings which had to be committed to memory. Informally he meditated with them, intimately teaching the disciples the body of truth which John recorded in his Gospel. John as a disciple of the Master presents Jesus as the Mediator. Furthermore, John presents the same Jesus as the other three evangelists do. "There is, in fact, no material difference in Christology between John and the three Synoptists."[42]

Looking at the whole problem of authorship from another angle, we may ask the question whether a disciple of John would have had the accurate topographical knowledge of Palestine which is revealed in the Fourth Gospel. Archaeologists have studied the places mentioned in the Gospel of John and come to the conclusion that the author of the Gospel had an accurate and personal knowledge of Palestinian geography. The location of Aenon near Salim (John 3:23) where John the Baptist was baptizing because "there were many waters there" has been verified. The pool of Bethesda (John 5:2) is described as having five porches; excavations in Jerusalem have brought to light the pool of Bethesda, with the five porches. The writer specifies the location of Bethany; it is fifteen furlongs from Jerusalem (John 11:18). Note that the writer uses the past tense in this verse: "Bethany *was* near to Jerusalem." The Roman armies had obliterated the little village so that it could no longer be found, yet by giving the exact distance in relation to Jerusalem, John tells the reader where he may find Bethany. The name Sychar, where Jesus met the woman at the well (John 4:5), has now been identified with Shechem. These two names must have been used synonymously because in the Old Syriac Version of the Gospel of John the name Shechem is used instead of Sychar, in John 4:5. Throughout the Gospel, all indications are that the author was a native of Palestine, who was there in person during Jesus' ministry and who

---

[42]F. F. Bruce, *The New Testament Documents; Are They Reliable?* Grand Rapids: Eerdmans, 5th Rev. Edition, 1965, p. 58.

could speak with personal knowledge of Palestine in the years after the fall of Jerusalem.

One last aspect must be seen while we view the totality of the authorship question. Many scholars have said that the Gospel of John has been heavily influenced by Greek culture, and that because of the concepts used in the Gospel it must have been written in a Greek environment. Of all the four Gospels, they said, the Fourth Gospel was really Hellenistic: there are definite indications of its affinity to Greek thought. However, this view is no longer tenable in the light of studies pertaining to the Dead Sea literature. Because of the light the Dead Sea Scrolls have cast upon the Gospel according to John, no one will dispute that the Fourth Gospel is essentially Palestinian. In fact, W. H. Brownlee comments: "If the Gospel as we know it was composed elsewhere, we must account for the migration of this thought and vocabulary."[43] The literature of the Dead Sea area has provided so many striking parallels with the Fourth Gospel that it is difficult to avoid the conclusion that in thought and language both originate in Palestine.

The Gospels provide the information that John the Baptist was born in the hills of Judea into a priestly family, that his parents were advanced in age when he was born, and that he spent his youth in the deserts until he began his prophetic work along the river Jordan (see especially Luke 1:80). Of course, it is difficult to tell what is meant by the expression "in the deserts," for it could easily refer to association with the people who lived near the Dead Sea and wrote the scrolls. Whether John the Baptist did actually live with the people of Qumran is hard to say. It is, however, virtually improbable that he had no knowledge of them at all, in view of the near proximity; he preached and baptized at the Jordan River only a few miles from the Qumran settlement. This does not imply that John the Baptist taught the same doctrine as the sectarians who lived at Qumran. A close analysis of the Dead Sea literature shows that the doctrine of the sectarians is different from the message proclaimed by John the Baptist near the Jordan. Yet the terminology used by the Baptist is the same as that of the people living in the Qumran settlement.

How is it possible that of the four Gospels that of John reveals close affinity in language and thought to the literature of the Dead Sea settlement? A possible answer to this question is that, according to John 1:35ff., some of Jesus' first disciples had followed John the Baptist. One of these former disciples of John and subsequently follower of Jesus has undoubtedly served as the channel through whom the Qumran terminology came into the Fourth Gospel. Presuming, for the

[43]*The Meaning of the Qumran Scrolls for the Bible.* New York: Oxford, 1964; p. 123.

moment, that this particular disciple, one of the twelve, is John the apostle, we have no difficulty understanding the affinity between Qumran and the Gospel of John.

Granted that the matter of authorship can never be fully settled, the traditional view that the author of the Fourth Gospel is John the apostle cannot be ignored, disregarded, or dealt with lightly. The traditional view, because of archaeology and recent literature discoveries simply cannot be dismissed as was done in the past. This view has merits of its own.

Sources

Did the author of the Fourth Gospel use any sources when he wrote his account? Some scholars say that he did, others that he did not. If the author did not rely upon any sources, did he have knowledge of the Gospel according to Matthew, according to Mark, according to Luke? What is the relationship of John's Gospel to that of the Synoptics?

Rudolf Bultmann says that the writer of the Fourth Gospel did not depend upon the Synoptics at all. Instead, Bultmann discovers a number of sources in this Gospel; he actually sees the Fourth Gospel as a cord made up of many strands. These strands must be separated so that we may learn how the writer put the Gospel together. Bultmann contends that the Gospel is a composition of Revelation speeches, interspersed with miracles, other sources and traditions, and concluded with a passion story. Bultmann is of the opinion that the Revelation speeches did not originate in Christianity but in the cultic sect of the first and second centuries called Gnosticism. Of course, the author of the Gospel of John Christianized all these speeches, and except for the introduction (the prologue), the author has put every speech into the mouth of Jesus; hence the name Revelation speeches. Some of the following passages, for example, are considered Relevation speeches: the prologue, most of Chapter 3, passages in Chapters 4 through 13, and most of Chapters 14 through 17. Incidentally, Bultmann has rearranged the text of the Fourth Gospel completely so that we cannot even speak of these passages and chapters in their customary sequence. Besides the Revelation speeches, the writer has made use of miracle stories. This is most evident, says Bultmann, in the overt references to the numerical order of these miracles. The changing of the water into wine is called "the first of the signs" (2:11) and the healing of the nobleman's son at Capernaum is called the second sign (4:54). These references are a clear indication that the writer leaned heavily on a document which had a list of miracle stories. Besides, he gained his material from other sources and traditions, such as the story about Jesus coming to Aenon near Salim where John the Baptist was baptizing (3:22-29). And finally, the author incorporated in his Gospel an independent account of the Passion.[44]

Whereas Bultmann maintains that the author of the Fourth Gospel did not have the accounts of the Synoptics before him but independent sources, a great number of scholars think that John did use the Gospel account of Matthew, Mark, and Luke in the composition of his Gospel. However, they are generally agreed that John depended mostly on Mark and to some extent on Luke, only a few think that he also used Matthew.[45] C. K. Barrett asserts that John relied on Mark and somewhat on Luke. He sees some parallelism between Mark and John in regard to the order of events listed. In total, he finds ten such incidents scattered through both Gospels. Discounting the introductory references to John the Baptist and the events of the Passion week, the incidents which follow each other directly in both Gospels are the feeding of the multitude and Jesus' walking on the Lake of Galilee.[46] The evidence advanced to show that John depended on the Second Gospel in the writing of his own is rather meager; the evidence to prove reliance on Luke's Gospel is even less significant.

Some scholars doubt whether John derived his material from any of the Synoptic writers. They rather see him work entirely independent of other sources. Says P. Gardner-Smith, "It is a fallacy, obvious yet strangely common, to think that he can only have learnt about the life of Christ and the incidents of the ministry from the perusal of some written document."[47] John must have had available to him an oral tradition which during the first century of the Christian era was rather influential and existed alongside the written Gospels. If John had access to the oral tradition, which in view of comments made by the church Fathers is most probable, the similarity in wording between John and the Synoptics can be explained. Though John agrees materially with the Gospels of Matthew, Mark, and Luke, he does not repeat but supplements. For this reason, the Fourth Gospel does not stand by itself but forms an integral part of the entire gospel tradition. This becomes clear when we look at the chronological framework of the Gospel of John and notice that the other three accounts can easily find a place within that framework. From the Synoptics we learn that Jesus' ministry may have been short, perhaps only one year because only one passover feast is mentioned. Yet when Jesus rebukes the people of Jerusalem for not having listened to him, "How often would I have gathered your

[44]R. Bultmann, The Gospel of John, pp. 6ff. Also see D. M. Smith, The Composition and Order of the Fourth Gospel. New Haven and London: Yale University Press, 1965.
[45]See, R. H. Lightfoot, St. John's Gospel. Oxford: University Press, 1960.
[46]Op. cit., pp. 34f.
[47]St. John and the Synoptic Gospels. Cambridge: University Press, 1938; p. xi.

children together" (Matt. 23:37 and Luke 13:34), the Synoptic writers seem to indicate that Jesus had visited the city of Jerusalem more often during his ministry. "But though the Synoptists give us these hints it is John alone who lets us see that Jesus came into conflict with the authorities in Jerusalem at an early date, and that this conflict was carried on at intervals through a ministry lasting at least three years."[48] In this connection we can understand that the witnesses at Jesus' trial could not agree on the wording of Jesus' statement that he would destroy the temple and in three days build another not made with hands (see Mark 14:58f.). According to John, Jesus spoke these words at the beginning of his ministry (John 2:19) and after three years those who had been called in to testify against Jesus could not remember the exact wording.

Eyewitness Account

One of the striking characteristics of the Gospel of John is the chronological framework, which not merely gives the reader the information that Jesus' ministry lasted three years but also provides the information of what happened in a succession of days; even the hour of day is mentioned a few times (see 1:39; 4:6, 52; 18:28; 19:14; and 20:19). In the first chapter of John's Gospel, the days are mentioned one by one in succession, and because it only takes about two days to travel from Bethany beyond the Jordan (1:28) to Galilee (2:1), indications are that the writer is speaking as an eyewitness who recollects what happened during the first part of Jesus' ministry. In fact, the phrase "and his disciples remembered" (2:17, 22) has every appearance of authenticity; an eyewitness recalls the incident of the temple cleansing.

According to John 3:23f., John (the Baptist) was baptizing in Aenon near Salim "because there was much water there." The exact location of these places has often been disputed and by many mapmakers has been placed north of Samaria about twenty-five miles south of the Lake of Galilee close to the river Jordan. Yet John 3:22 provides the information that Jesus and his disciples came into the land of Judea, and travelled to where John was baptizing. "The location of Salim may now be regarded as reasonably certain. Three miles east of Shechem lies the ancient town of Salim of which traces survive in Israelite, Hellenistic and Samaritan literature. And near Salim lies *Ainun* with a name undoubtedly derived from the Aramaic *Ainon* meaning 'little fountain.' Since these two places lie near the head-waters of the *Wadi Far'ah*, with many springs in the vicinity, St. John might well declare that

---

'there were many waters there.' "[49] From there, Jesus went to Sychar at the site of Jacob's well. The writer of the Fourth Gospel describes in detail the characteristics of that place: "Sir, . . . the well is deep"; "our fathers worshipped in this mountain [Gerizim]"; and "the fields white to the harvest." The reader cannot suppress the conclusion that someone who was personally present as an eyewitness is relating the account.

Also, in Chapter 4 of the Gospel of John, the topographical knowledge of the writer is evident in the scene of the healing of the nobleman's son. This high-ranking officer lived in Capernaum, a city along the northwestern shore of the Lake of Galilee, a place well below sea-level. When he heard that Jesus had arrived in Cana, a town in the mountains of Galilee some twenty-five miles southwest of Capernaum, he had to ascend from a place far below sea level to a place high above sea level. Three times the writer of the Fourth Gospel uses the preposition *down* to indicate the descent in the road which Jesus would have to travel in order to reach Capernaum. "(The official) begged him to come *down* and heal his son." "Sir, come *down* before my child dies." "As he was going *down*, his servants met him." Here speaks the voice of someone who has intimate knowledge of that area.

Throughout the Gospel, many direct and indirect references reveal that the writer was an eyewitness. Even though many scholars reject this evidence in the Fourth Gospel, it is unrealistic to expect more from the author.[50] Raymond E. Brown sums it up rather succinctly as follows: "When all is said and done, the combination of external and internal evidence associating the Fourth Gospel with John son of Zebedee makes this the strongest hypothesis, if one is prepared to give credence to the Gospel's claim of an eyewitness source."[51]

John and Recent Manuscripts

Though the Gospel of John has its setting in Palestine, it was nevertheless written in Greek and according to tradition in the city of Ephesus. For this reason, C. H. Dodd maintained that the links between the Fourth Gospel and Hellenism are strong; the Greek influence could be ascertained in vocabulary and thought. Some scholars wished to see similarity between the use of *Logos* in John and its use in Hellenic thought. Others saw traces of Gnosticism in John's Gospel. Especially Rudolf Bultmann taught that the writer of the Fourth Gospel had Christianized Gnostic teachings; Gnosticism arose in the first

---

[49]A. M. Hunter, *According to John*. Philadelpia: Westminster, 1968, pp. 50f.
[50]Morris, *op. cit.*, p. 208.
[51]*The Anchor Bible, The Gospel According to John* (i-xii), Garden City, N.Y.: Doubleday, 1966, p. xcviii.

century after Christ and taught a dualism dividing the spiritual and the material — the spiritual is good, the material bad.

However, since the discovery of the Gnostic library at Nag Hammadi in southern Egypt in the year 1946, much light has been cast on the relationship of Gnosticism to Christianity. From the books found at Nag Hammadi, the evidence shows that John did not borrow Gnostic thought which he tried to Christianize; rather the opposite has happened. Gnostic teachers of the second century assimilated the teaching of John's Gospel into their system, so that Gnosticism truly became a Christian heresy.[52]

And because of the discoveries of the documents near the Dead Sea, the opinion that the Gospel of John has a Greek background had to be revised completely. In fact, because of the findings of the Dead Sea Scrolls, the Fourth Gospel literally has been brought back to its cradle in Palestine. Geographically, the settlement of Khirbet Qumran where the scrolls were written, and the area where Jesus performed his ministry are contiguous. The similarity in wording is often striking, so that there is a definite relationship between the Qumran scrolls and the Gospel of John. To take only one example: In the first chapter of John's Gospel, the priests and Levites from Jerusalem ask John the Baptist, "Who are you?" John tells them that he is neither the Christ nor Elijah nor the prophet. But he says: "I am the voice of one crying in the wilderness, 'Make straight the way of the Lord,' as the prophet Isaiah said" (v. 23).

The reference to Isaiah 40:3 is also found in the Manual of Discipline which constituted the book of rules for the inhabitants of Qumran. In the section about the appointment of elders in the Qumran community (1QS 8:13-15), the following rule is given: "When these men exist in Israel, these are the provisions whereby they are to be kept apart from any consort with froward men, to the end that they may indeed 'go into the wilderness to prepare the way,' i.e., do what Scripture enjoins when it says, 'Prepare in the wilderness the way . . . make straight in the desert a highway for our God' (Isa. 40:3). The reference into the study of the Law which God commanded through Moses to the end that as occasion arises, all things may be done in accordance with what is revealed therein and with what the prophets also have revealed through God's holy spirit."[53]

The Gospel of John describes the contrasts of life and death, of truth and the lie, of spirit and the flesh, of light and darkness. These

---

[52]R. E. Brown, "The Gospel of Thomas and St. John's Gospel." *New Testament Studies* 9 (1962-1963), pp. 155-177.
[53]T. H. Gaster, *The Scriptures of the Dead Sea Sect.* London: Secker & Warburg; 1957, p. 65.

contrasts are also common to the literature of Qumran, which in effect places the Gospel of John in the context of Palestinian Judaism, not in first-century Hellenism or second-century Gnosticism. Hence Jean Danielou concludes: "This is a discovery of capital importance which shows that the backdrop of John's thought is Jewish, and thereby a breach is made in the theses put forth by the two most important recent commentators on John: Dodd, who interprets him as stemming from Hellenism; and Bultmann, who links him to the Gnostics."[54] In short, Hellenic thought and Gnostic terminology is really Jewish and first-century Palestinian at that. Though the Gospel of John and the Qumran scrolls differ considerably in interpretation and application of the Old Testament, they do have a common background in the Scriptures and theology of the Old Testament.

As is evident throughout the Qumran scrolls, the Old Testament is used in support of a rigorous system of work righteousness in the Qumran community. In contrast, John uses the Old Testament to lead men to Christ, the fulfillment of prophecy. The writers of the scrolls wrote so that men might keep the Law and obtain salvation; John wrote to reveal Christ, so that whoever believes in Him may not perish but have life eternal. Thus, even though parallelisms between the Dead Sea Scrolls and the Gospel of John are striking, the Fourth Gospel is not an outgrowth of Qumran sectarianism. In John's Gospel Christ occupies the central place, for, in fact, it is the gospel of Jesus Christ according to John.

---

[54]*The Dead Sea Scrolls and Primitive Christianity*. Baltimore: Helicon Press, 1958; p. 108.

7. THEOLOGY

The literature on Biblical theology in respect to the four Gospels is phenomenal. Theologians have touched on every topic conceivable; topics which belong to another age have been re-examined, and questions which at one time were answered are once again fully discussed. Because of their writings, theologians have placed theology in a prominent position.

The theologian of today is not at all averse to leaving his carrel in the stack room of the library and talk about theology to people who are not his colleagues and students. He converses freely with people who have a vital interest in theology but lack a theological training. He engages in discussions on the person of Jesus; he exchanges his views on the resurrection, and with Christian lawyers and Jewish Rabbis debates the trial of Jesus.

In this chapter, three of these topics are discussed, not exhaustively but as subjects representing current issues. The first topic, which has thus far produced a flood of books and articles, centers on the title *Son of Man*. Does this title originate with Jesus or did the early Christian community attribute this name to him? Does this name refer to Jesus or to a person distinct from and other than Jesus? Is this title authentic? These are some of the questions raised in the "Son of Man" debate.

A second topic of interest touches on the title *Son of God*. A subject of this nature evokes the interest of every Christian; carefully we examine the record, the documentary evidence, the questions and the conclusion. To a large extent, we seek to answer the query: Was Jesus of Nazareth really the Son of God?

The third topic can be summarized in the word *resurrection*. Of course, the subject pertains to the resurrection of Jesus. The meaning of his resurrection, the question of the empty tomb, understanding the resurrection today — all these are part of the discussion. Of the three

131

topics which we have selected for this chapter on theology, the topic on the resurrection is most vital: it is the basis of the Christian's faith.

We begin with the topic of the Son of Man debate and listen to the answers given to the questions raised. Next, we attend the "trial" of Jesus and learn from the evidence presented whether Jesus of Nazareth is the Son of God. And last, we examine the Easter events which describe the resurrection of Jesus.

I. SON OF MAN

Source

The title *Son of man* is actually limited to the four Gospels. Outside of the Gospels it occurs once in the book of Acts. Stephen in his dying moment, seeing the glory of God and Jesus standing at the right hand of God, said: "Behold, I see the heavens opened, and the Son of man standing at the right hand of God" (Acts 7:56). The title never occurs in any of the New Testament epistles (except for the quotation from Psalm 8:4 in Hebrews 2:6, which has no bearing at all on the discussion). The saying occurs twice in the book of Revelation in the form of allusions to Daniel 7:9, 13. The first time, it occurs in the context of John's vision on the island of Patmos. He heard a voice, saw seven golden lampstands, "and in the midst of the lampstands one like a son of man" (1:13; see Daniel 7:9). The second reference alludes to Daniel 7:13, "with the clouds of heaven there came one like a son of man." John, in Revelation 14:14, says, "Then I looked, and lo, a white cloud, and seated on the cloud one like a son of man."

The textual evidence for the name *Son of man* lies in the four Gospels. To be precise, the evidence is found in the sayings of Jesus recorded in the Gospels of Matthew, Mark, Luke, and John. In total, the number of times the expression *Son of man* occurs is about equally divided among the four evangelists. It occurs sixty-nine times in the Synoptic Gospels and thirteen times in John's Gospel. Eliminating the parallels in the Gospels of Matthew, Mark, and Luke, we bring the total of sixty-nine down to thirty-eight. If we add to this number the total of the Fourth Gospel, we come to fifty-one times that Jesus speaks of himself as the Son of man.[1]

The expression itself originates in the Aramaic language, not the Greek. Because of this, some scholars have suggested that the expression is another way of referring to man in general. But this can hardly be the case because the Gospels intimate that the expression is used as a

---

[1] J. Jeremias, *New Testament Theology*. New York: Charles Scribner's Sons, 1971; pp. 259f.

title. The words of Matthew 26:24 provide the evidence, "The Son of man goes as it is written of him, but woe to that man by whom the Son of man is betrayed! It would have been better for that man if he had not been born." Two expressions are used in this text side by side: "Son of man" and "man." Neither of the two refers to man in general. The expression *"Son of man"* refers to Jesus and that of *"man"* to Judas.

A more plausible observation is that in Aramaic the words *Son of man* were used by a speaker to refer modestly to himself. Instead of saying: "I am going to Jerusalem," Jesus would say in harmony with the customs of his day: "the Son of man goes to Jerusalem." For example, in Matthew 16:13 Jesus asks the disciples: "Who do men say that the Son of man is?" This same question in the parallel accounts of Mark 8:27 and Luke 9:18 reads: "Who do men say that I am?" and "Who do the people say that I am?"

Setting

The fact that the title *Son of man* is found only in the Gospels and never in the Epistles is telling. Besides that, the title in the Gospels comes only from the lips of Jesus. John 12:34 forms no exception to this because the crowd in asking a question is only repeating what Jesus said: "How can you say that the Son of man must be lifted up?" The setting for the saying "Son of man" points to a Palestinian context. Undoubtedly, Paul must have been familiar with the expression, yet he does not use it in his epistles as a title for Jesus. Only in Stephen's speech does the saying occur. But this instance only strengthens the contention that the usage points to a Palestinian context. "The use of the title Son of man is thus pre-Pauline, and the title began to be avoided soon after the transition from a Semitic to a Greek-speaking milieu. The reason is easy to discover; the intention was to avoid the danger that native Greeks would take the title as a designation of descent. It continued only in the Palestinian Jewish-Christian community (Acts 7:56; Gospel of the Hebrews; Hegesippus); here there was no fear of misunderstanding."[2]

In view of the fact that the expression *"Son of man"* is used exclusively by Jesus, the early church must have preserved the sayings of Jesus. No one calls Jesus "Son of man" in the Gospels; it is only Jesus himself who uses this title to refer to himself. For that reason, the early church considered the title to belong to Jesus.

How did Jesus use the expression? Scholars have divided the sayings of Jesus in which the title *Son of man* occurs in three categories: first, the group of sayings relating to Jesus' earthly ministry ("The Son of

---

[2]Jeremias, *ibid.,* p. 265.

man has authority on earth to forgive sin," Mark 2:10, "and is Lord of the sabbath," Mark 2:28); second, the group of sayings which speak of the suffering, death, and resurrection of the Son of man ("the Son of man must suffer many things, and be rejected by the elders and the chief priests and the scribes, and be killed, and after three days rise again" Mark 8:31); and third, the group of sayings in which the future coming and exaltation of the Son of man is expressed ("For whoever is ashamed of me and of my words in this adulterous and sinful generation, of him will the Son of man also be ashamed, when he comes in the glory of his Father with the holy angels," Mark 8:38).

Interpretation

How are the sayings of Jesus relating to his earthly ministry interpreted? Some scholars readily employ form critical methods and claim that the texts which have the expression *"Son of man"* are a product of the early Christian community.[3] Not Jesus spoke the words, but the early church attributed the words to Jesus. Let us look at the text in which Jesus says that the Son of man has authority on earth to forgive sin (Mark 2:10), that the Son of man is Lord of the sabbath (Mark 2:28), that the Son of man is a friend of tax collectors and sinners (Matt. 11:19), and that the Son of man has nowhere to lay his head (Matt. 8:20). Form critics say that Mark 2:10 definitely is a product of the early church because of the break in the story. "But that you may know that the Son of man has authority on earth to forgive sins" — he said to the paralytic — "I say to you, rise, take up your pallet and go home" (Mark 2:10f.). Because of this break in thought, many scholars claim that the expression *"Son of man"* must be an addition to the original story.

However, Miss Morna D. Hooker observes, "Any attempt to dismiss this saying, either in part or *in toto,* as a creation of the early Church, can, unless it looks beyond this passage, be criticized for failing to take account of all the facts. For the absence of the phrase 'Son of man' in other passages where it might well have been introduced by those who did not grasp its meaning is quite as significant as its isolated appearances in Mark 2."[4] If the form and redaction critics maintain that because of the break in the construction the Son of man saying must be considered an addition, they will also have to explain why the parallel passages in Matthew and Luke have the anacoluthon (the

---

[3]R. Bultmann, *The History of the Synoptic Tradition.* New York: Harper & Row, 1963. M. Dibelius, *From Tradition to Gospel.* London: Nicholson & Warren, 1934. Also see H. Conzelmann, *An Outline of the Theology of the New Testament.* London: SCM, 1969. G. Bornkamm, *Jesus of Nazareth.* H. E. Todt, *The Son of Man in the Synoptic Tradition.* Philadelphia: Westminster, 1965.
[4]*The Son of Man in Mark.* London: S.P.C.K., 1967; p. 83.

grammatical break) and the Son of man saying (Matt. 9:6, Luke 5:24). If all three evangelists have the same wording and grammatical construction, there is every reason to believe that the words go back to an original source, to Jesus Christ himself.

Moreover, why would the early Christian community change the wording? In the context of the Gospel account, Jesus frequently finds himself in the company of tax collectors and sinners (Matt. 11:19). To say that the early church put the words "Son of man" on the lips of Jesus does not seem at all in harmony with the rest of the Gospel account.

And what about the words of Matthew 11:19 (and its parallel in Luke 7:34)? Is there any evidence that Jesus could not have spoken these words "the Son of man came eating and drinking, and they say, 'Behold, a glutton and a drunkard, a friend of tax collectors and sinners' "? All the evidence seems to indicate that these words are authentic because there is no compelling reason to think otherwise. In a penetrating study on the Son of man sayings in the Synoptic Gospels, I. Howard Marshall says: "Since it is extremely unlikely that the early church would have invented the comparison between John and Jesus found in Luke vii.33f. or created such scurrilous comments about him, there is every reason to accept the content of this saying as genuine."[5]

Then there are the sayings which refer to the suffering, death, and resurrection of the Son of man. They are found in texts such as Mark 8:31; 9:31; and 10:33f. Mark 8:31 is representative of the other two. "And he began to teach them that the Son of man must suffer many things, and be rejected by the elders and the chief priests and the scribes, and be killed, and after three days rise again." Again the form and redaction critics reject the genuineness of these sayings. They assert that all references to the passion of Jesus must date from a period after Easter. Hence, we have in these texts history presented in the form of prophecy — prophecy on the basis of an actual event directed backward. Bultmann rejects the authenticity of these sayings because he maintains that not Jesus but the early Christian community "predicted" his suffering and death.[6] Says Günther Bornkamm, "Even if we do not doubt that Jesus reckoned on his violent death, these prophecies of his suffering and resurrection can hardly be considered to be Jesus' own words. They presume a detailed knowledge of the Passion and Easter story."[7]

But are these sayings so foreign to Jesus that they must be assigned

[5]"The Synoptic Son of Man Sayings in Recent Discussion." New Testament Studies 12 (4,1966), pp. 339f. Also see C. Colpe, "Son of Man." Theol. Worterbuch Zum N.T., Vol. 8, p. 434.
[6]Theology of the New Testament, Vol. 1. New York: Scribner's, 1952; pp. 29ff.
[7]Jesus of Nazareth, p. 229.

to the Christian community of first-century Palestine? The context of Mark 8:31 indicates that the saying is an integral part of the Gospel account. And the broader context of Scripture supports the elements in the text. For example, the concept "to be rejected" was not at all unfamiliar to Jesus and his audience because of Psalm 118:22, "The stone which the builders rejected has become the head of the corner." In the passion week, Jesus referred to and quoted this very passage from the psalms (Mark 12:10). Again, the objection to Jesus using the expression *"Son of man"* in these sayings loses validity in the light of the context of the passage.

Finally, there are the passages which speak about the coming of the Son of man in glory. They are Mark 8:38; 13:26; 14:62; Matthew 24:27, 37, 39, 44. These passages have all been accepted as genuine. No form critic demurs; no redaction critic objects to their validity. They are authentic because Jesus himself spoke these words about the future coming of the Son of man.

Understanding these texts, however, is another story. Take for example Mark 8:38. Jesus says, "For whoever is ashamed of me and of my words in this adulterous and sinful generation, of him will the Son of man also be ashamed, when he comes in the glory of his Father with the holy angels." Who is this Son of man? Certainly not, say the form critic and the redaction critic, Jesus of Nazareth. "Striking is here the distinction between the 'I' of the earthly Jesus and the Son of man who is to come."[8] But does Jesus really refer to a person other than himself? Does this person called Son of man supersede him? Do the passages in context really prove that Jesus does not refer to himself when he uses the title *Son of man*? If the early church, according to the form and redaction critics, ascribed the title *Son of man* to Jesus in passages relating to his earthly ministry, does Jesus in these passages refer to a second Son of man? Are there two Sons of man? The questions can be multiplied, but the point at issue is whether Jesus speaks about himself as the future Son of man.

In Mark 8:38 and its parallels, it is not a question of two persons but rather of one person in two conditions. Jesus is talking about his earthly state contrasted to his heavenly state. "A possible line of interpretation is that he was saying that a person who confessed him, an apparently lowly person proclaiming the message of God, will be confessed by him when he appears as witness and judge at the last judgment in glory. The saying would then express pointedly the contrast between the present lowly condition of Jesus as 'I' and his future glory as the Son of man."[9]

---

[8]*Ibid.*, p. 228. Also see R. Bultmann, *History*, pp. 122f.
[9]I. H. Marshall, "Synoptic Son of Man Sayings," p. 345. See also I. H. Marshall,

Meaning

When Jesus used the title *Son of man,* he stood within the tradition of Scripture. That is, he spoke in terms of Daniel 7, where the author writes, "I saw in the night visions, and behold, with the clouds of heaven there came one like a son of man, and he came to the Ancient of Days and was presented before him. And to him was given dominion and glory and kingdom, that all peoples, nations, and languages should serve him; his dominion is an everlasting dominion, which shall not pass away, and his kingdom one that shall not be destroyed" (vv. 13, 14).

Jesus, therefore, did not see another person bearing the name *Son of man.* "In that case, one would have to suppose that Jesus had seen himself as a forerunner, as the prophet of the Son of man."[10] Jesus came to fulfill the Old Testament prophecies, and Daniel 7:13f. was one of them.

The question arises, how the crowds surrounding Jesus during his earthly ministry understood the expression *"Son of man"* when Jesus applied the prophetic words of Daniel 7 to himself. This question must be answered with reference to his teaching on the Kingdom of God. When he taught the crowds that the Kingdom of God was near, he directly and indirectly taught the fulfillment of Daniel's prophecy. And in this Kingdom of God, the Son of man occupied a central place. For Jesus, the Kingdom of God had fully arrived when he told the disciples of John the Baptist to look around and see the blind seeing, the lame walking, the lepers cleansed, the deaf hearing, the dead raised, and the poor hearing the gospel (Matt. 11:4f.).

Jesus appeared among his fellow men as the Son of man. Yet it is rather significant that Jesus in his Son of man sayings never speaks of the second coming of this person. The coming of Jesus, born as a human being, called Son of man, is never regarded as the parousia (the second coming). Jesus regarded his work as Son of man in his earthly ministry and in his heavenly exaltation as a unit.[11]

This unit consists of two levels: Jesus' earthly ministry and Jesus' exaltation in heaven. Not only the Synoptic Gospel writers teach this truth; also John in the Fourth Gospel brings out this same teaching. Perhaps John is even more explicit than the other three evangelists in revealing the meaning of the expression *"Son of man."* Stephen S. Smalley in a study on the Son of man sayings in the Fourth Gospel observes, "It is the Fourth Evangelist in particular who has an eye to

---

"The Son of Man in Contemporary Debate." *Evangelical Quarterly* 42 (2, 1970); pp. 74ff.
[10]J. Jeremias, *New Testament Theology,* p. 276.
[11]O. Cullmann, *The Christology of the New Testament.* Philadelphia: Westminster, 1959; p. 160.

the 'two-level' character of this identity, earthly and heavenly; for it is he who draws out for his readers so clearly the conjunction between these two levels in the person of the Son of man himself."[12] It goes without saying that the relationship between the terms Son of man and Son of God is very close. Especially in the Fourth Gospel, the writer focuses attention on the identity of Jesus: he is Son of man and Son of God.

Not without significance is the use of the double definite article in the expression "*the* Son of *the* man" as it occurs in Aramaic and its sister dialects. The term shows the fulness of the humanity which Jesus assumed when he was born. And because the term is Jesus' favorite self-designation, it gives unity to Scripture: Jesus took upon himself humanity in its fullest sense and appeared as the visible image of God. "He who has seen me has seen the Father" (John 14:9). "Hence only Jesus Christ, the second man, is the image of God in a full and final sense. In the fulness of time he appeared as the visible image of the invisible God (II Cor. 4:4ff.), and as the beginning of a new humanity to restore God's marred image in us."[13] By using the term as a self-designation, Jesus indicates that he reaches back to the beginning of human history and forward to man's restoration.

In this brief survey of the vast field of this particular topic, we have merely presented a bird's eye view. We have shown the various facets of the expression used by Jesus during his ministry, and we have tried to show that the saying "*Son of man*" was spoken by Jesus himself. Problems remain and questions unanswered in regard to this title. We conclude with the observation of Joachim Jeremias, "the title was rooted in the tradition of the sayings of Jesus right from the beginning; as a result, it was sacrosanct, and no-one dared to eliminate it. That means that the apocalyptic Son of Man sayings which we have recognized as the earliest stratum must in essentials go back to Jesus himself."[14]

II. SON OF GOD

Throughout the Gospels no mention is made of anyone questioning Jesus' use of the term "*Son of man.*" When he in the last day of his earthly life applied the term "*son of God*" to himself, his hearers reacted sharply and spoke of blasphemy. In the trial of Jesus before the Jewish Sanhedrin, the expression "*Son of God*" stands out in bold relief.

---

[12]"The Johannine Son of Man Sayings" *New Testament Studies* 15 (3, 1969), p. 299.
[13]E. Stauffer, *New Testament Theology*. London: SCM, 1963; p. 111.
[14]*New Testament Theology*, pp. 266f.

Son

Whereas the self-designation *"Son of man"* is found very frequently throughout the four Gospels, the expression *"Son of God"* does not come from the lips of Jesus. That does not mean, however, that the term *"Son"* is never used. In numerous instances Jesus reveals the Father-Son relationship, especially in the Gospel of John. In the Synoptic Gospels, these two texts reveal the intimacy of the Father to the Son: "All things have been delivered to me by my Father; and no one knows the Son except the Father, and no one knows the Father except the Son and any one to whom the Son chooses to reveal him" (Matt. 11:27), and "But of that day or that hour no one knows, not even the angels in heaven, nor the Son, but only the Father" (Mark 13:32).

The first of these two texts has been called in doubt ever since the rise of form criticism because the historical Jesus could not have spoken these words.[15] Bultmann believes with Dibelius that the saying is a Hellenistic Revelation which, because of its similarity to the words of Matthew 28:18 ("All authority in heaven and on earth has been given to me"), has been regarded as a saying of the risen Lord.

The second text (Mark 13:32) also has lost its validity as a statement of Jesus. This saying, according to the form critics, is actually a reflection of the christology of the early Christian church. The text is considered to be a Jewish saying found at the end of a Jewish Apocalypse, which Luke for dogmatic reasons omitted. "Infrequently though the Messianic title Son (of God) is found in the references to himself of the historical Jesus, the more its use can be explained from the Credo of the Church in which it has its own secure place — based on Ps. ii.7."[16]

The reason why Bultmann and his followers do not attribute these passages to Jesus but to the early Christian community, and why they make a distinction between Jesus and the risen Lord can be seen in a comment made by Hans Conzelmann, "The meaning is that during his lifetime, Jesus was the Messiah (Son of David); after his death, he was appointed by God to be Son of God. This sonship of God is understood in legal, and not in physical terms. The formula does not distinguish two 'natures,' but two stages in the existence of Jesus. There is no knowledge of pre-existence. As Messiah, Jesus was not a supernatural being, but a man with a particular status."[17] Bultmann himself, however, questions whether Jesus was conscious of his Messiahship; he

---

[15]See M. Dibelius, *From Tradition to Gospel,* pp. 279ff. R. Bultmann, *History,* pp. 159ff.

[16]G. Bornkamm, *Jesus of Nazareth,* p. 226.

[17]*Outline,* p. 77.

rather understands belief in the Messiahship as a consequence of the belief in the resurrection.

Title

What does Bultmann do with the title *Son of God*? He will have to reckon with the words of Psalm 2:7, "He said to me, 'You are my son, today I have begotten you.'" He asserts that in Judaism and in the Christian church the title was applied to the king. Though in Judaism and the church the title has not been interpreted mythologically, this was the case in Hellenistic Christianity where it was applied to the Messiah as a super-natural being, the Son of God. The passages in the Gospels of Matthew, Mark, and Luke which mention the title *Son of God* are a reflection of their Hellenistic-Christian origin. The account of Jesus' transfiguration in which the voice from heaven says, "this is my beloved son" (Mark 9:7) must be traced to an early tradition. Bultmann calls this early tradition "an Easter-story projected backward into Jesus' lifetime." So is Peter's confession: "You are the Christ, the Son of the living God" (Matt. 16:16). The account of the Jesus' baptism in which the heavenly voice calls Jesus "my beloved son" (Matt. 3:17) is regarded as a legend.[18]

Though Jesus does not call himself Son of God in the Gospel accounts, those surrounding him do. From every direction he is recognized as divine: a voice from heaven, satan, demons, his disciples, and the Roman centurion. Is it possible and necessary to deny these references historical significance?

In the temptation account, in his confrontation with the demons, and in his conversations with his disciples, Jesus does not establish his divine descent. The question is not whether he is the Son of God and therefore able to do miracles. Rather, it is a question of obedient sonship. What is crucial in all these passages is whether Jesus as the Son of God demonstrates his obedience to the Father. Would he submit to the agony and suffering lying before him? His ability to perform miracles is not at stake. But, as the Son of God, is he going to withstand satan's temptations, the demons' interrogations, and the disciples' aspirations? Is he, as the Son of God, obedient to his Father and conscious of his calling?

The answers are affirmative. "On the other hand, from the moment of his baptism the consciousness of the closest oneness with the Father always accompanies Jesus. It is certainly no accident that the words from heaven at the transfiguration partially repeat those of the heavenly voice at the baptism."[19] It is God the Father who at the time of Jesus'

---

[18]*Theology*, Vol. 2. pp. 26f., and p. 50.
[19]O. Cullmann, *Christology*, pp. 284f.

baptism and transfiguration affirms the Father-Son relationship. Therefore, to say that these events did not occur but are stories projected
back into the life-time of Jesus is dubious and improbable.

Is there any compelling reason not to accept as genuine the passages
in which Jesus himself speaks about his sonship? In Matthew 11:27
and Mark 13:32, Jesus speaks about his relationship to the Father as
his Son. When we see the unique relationship of Father and Son in
these passages, the texts become meaningful. In the context of the rest
of the New Testament, these verses are an integral part; nothing speaks
against their authenticity. For example, in Acts 1:7 Jesus tells the
disciples that it is the Father who fixes the times and seasons by his
own authority.

Thus far we have only looked at the evidence provided by the Synoptic Gospels. We have not said anything about the numerous references
to the divine sonship of Jesus recorded in the Fourth Gospel.

John's Gospel

Numerous are the texts that speak about the relationship of Father
and Son in the Fourth Gospel. Already in the Prologue, John says,
"we have beheld his glory, glory as of the only Son from the Father
(1:14). In the discourse following the feeding of the five thousand,
Jesus says to the Jews, "For this is the will of my Father, that every
one who sees the Son and believes in him should have eternal life; and
I will raise him up at the last day" (6:40). And in the so-called High-
priestly Prayer, Jesus prays, "Father, the hour has come, glorify thy
Son that the Son may glorify thee" (17:1). These passages are representative of the Father-Son motif in John's Gospel.

How does the modern theologian understand the references to Father
and Son? To him, these references are merely a reflection of the early
Christian theology which the early church had developed as a confession
of faith. The church of that day confessed that Jesus was the Son of
God the Father. John's Prologue, which has the phrase "only Son
from the Father" (1:14), is such a confession. Says Rudolf Bultmann,
"It is the community that is speaking! And in what way? In its form
the Prologue is a piece of *cultic-liturgical poetry,* oscillating between
the languages of revelation and confession."[20] Bultmann, therefore, concludes that the writer of the Fourth Gospel has taken a hymn used by
the early Christian community in worship services and has developed it
with some comments of his own in the form of a Prologue to his Gospel
(1:1-18).

Questions concerning the pre-existent state of the Son of God and

---

[20]*The Gospel of John.* Philadelphia: Westminster, 1971; p. 14.

the subsequent virgin birth are considered irrelevant because Bultmann simply rejects such teaching. "John has no theory about the pre-existent one's miraculous manner of entry into the world nor about the manner of his union with the man Jesus. He knows neither the legend of the virgin birth nor that of Jesus' birth in Bethlehem — or if he knows of them, he will have nothing to do with them. Jesus comes from Nazareth, and this fact, offensive to 'the Jews,' is emphasized (1:45; 7:52) rather than deprecated."[21] Jesus is genuinely man; he came into the world as a human being. What about his divinity? That, according to Bultmann, did not become visible at all to his disciples. His divinity lies in his mission: he brought the revelation of God and as such was himself revelation. As the bearer of revelation Jesus is able to see through man, and man is confronted with divine revelation.

The frequently occurring address "Father" does not differ at all from the teachings of the Old Testament and the Jewish Rabbis. If we may speak of a difference, says the modern theologian, we must see that the Father-Son relationship is expressed in the Old Testament and in Jewish thought not in terms of birth but in terms of election. The nation Israel is called God's first-born son (Exod. 4:22). That is, God elected Israel to that unique and favored position: Israel, God's Son. And the prophet Jeremiah records the word of the Lord saying, "I am a father to Israel and Ephraim is my firstborn" (31:9). Likewise, the words of Psalm 2:7, quoted in the New Testament with reference to the Messiah, do not speak of a divine birth but of a king who transfers his rights to his son. "I will tell of the decree of the Lord! He said to me, 'You are my son, today I have begotten you.' "

The Jews saw a relation between the individual who trusted in God and God who embraced the righteous person in the nation Israel. The relationship, therefore, was not considered collectively for the nation but individually for the faithful. "Jesus' use of the name 'Father' for God cannot therefore be taken as the introduction of a new idea of God. It reveals peculiarities, however, which have the closest connection with Jesus' message as a whole. It is significant that the father-son relationship is nowhere applied to the nation, just as Jesus certainly never refers to the nation and its history as a guarantee of redemption."[22] Jesus saw the presence of God as a father providing for his children. Thus Jesus could say that the Father makes his sun to rise on the evil and the good (Matt. 5:45).

The modern theologian aptly points to the teaching of the Old Testa-

---

[21]*Theology*, Vol. II, p. 41. Also see Bultmann, *Gospel*, p. 59 n. 5. C. H. Dodd, *The Interpretation of the Fourth Gospel*. New York: Cambridge, 1953; p. 260.
[22]G. Bornkamm, *Jesus of Nazareth*, p. 126. And see Bultmann, *Theology*, Vol. I, p. 23.

ment and the theology of the Jewish Rabbis, but he is obliged to say something positive about the teaching of the New Testament as well. In the Gospel of John, Jesus is presented as the Son sent by the Father. "And the Father who sent me has himself borne witness to me" (5:37). The recurring theme in the Fourth Gospel is that Jesus is the Father's delegate, sent by God, speaking in behalf of God, as God's representative among men.

Confidently and factually the modern theologian speaks about the Father-Son relationship in the Gospel of John. With reference to the Prologue of the Fourth Gospel, Hans Conzelmann is of the opinion that positing two divine beings (Father and Son) next to each other is a mythological conception. Does John really intend to teach that the Son is a divine being next to God? What does John mean when he says that the Word was with God, and the Word was God? (1:1). According to Conzelmann, John does not present Jesus as a divine being next to God, but as a representative in behalf of God. When man sees the Son, he is seeing the Father. Man is asked to believe in the Son; when he accepts the Son in faith, he realizes that God has sent the Son to work out his plan of salvation. When man believes in the Son, he is able to see the Father, in faith. "The key-words 'sending,' 'the one who is sent' (emissary) mean that God himself is responsible for salvation (3:16; Rom. 8:32, 39 shows the connection with tradition). Because Jesus is the one who is sent, and is otherwise nothing, he is one with the Father. Their unity is the unity of the saving work."[23] God has commissioned Jesus to call man to faith. When man responds to this call and accepts the Son, he at the same time accepts the Father. In the work of salvation, the Father and the Son are one.

Though the modern theologian has explained the Father-Son relationship with the aid of a few Scriptural references, he has failed to explain the relationship exegetically. And for this reason, his arguments are far from convincing.

Evaluation

What, in fact, does the writer of the Fourth Gospel say? In the numerous references to the Father-Son relationship, he makes it very clear that this relationship is unique: the Son came forth out of the Father and came into the world. John records the words of Jesus which speak of heavenly origin, "I came from the Father and have come into the world; again, I am leaving the world and going to my Father" (16:28). In the original Greek, the construction shows that Jesus came *out of* the Father; Jesus had his origin in the very being of the Father.

---

[23]H. Conzelmann, *Outline*, p. 341.

Leon Morris, in commenting on this particular verse says, "Here we have the great movement of salvation. It is a twofold movement, from heaven to earth and back again. Christ's heavenly origin is important, else He could not be the Saviour of men. But His heavenly destination is also important, for it witnesses to the Father's seal on the Son's saving work."[24]

Jesus, according to John's record, always pointed to his heavenly origin. Thus he could say to the Jews, "You are from below, I am from above; you are of this world, I am not of this world" (8:23). Jesus belongs to the "above." He did not receive God's approval by being a righteous person who because of the Father's approval might be called Son of God. Jesus says repeatedly that he came from heaven to earth: "for I know whence I have come and whither I am going" (8:14). In this same chapter, John transmits the discourse of Jesus and the Jews in which Jesus unmistakably refers to his divine origin, "If God were your Father, you would love me, for I proceed and came forth from God; I came not of my own accord, but he sent me" (8:42). Again, the Greek indicates that Jesus proceeds *out of* God; he comes forth out of the very being of God.[25] "The author of John so strongly emphasizes the fact of Jesus' origin in the Father that he never even asks whether it is compatible with human birth of known parents (John 7:27) from Nazareth (John 1:45; 7:41f.). For him Jesus' direct birth from God stands above his earthly birth."[26]

Of course, the modern theologian has taken note of the passages in the Gospel of John which refer to the divine origin of the Son of God. However, he places these particular passages in his own frame of thinking. For Bultmann, the teaching of the pre-existence of Christ as well as the teaching of the virgin birth are not rooted in history but in Gnostic mythology. "It is not only that Jesus' equality with God is asserted of his actions as well as his words. it is also that Jesus' words of authority are not interpreted in terms of election, vocation and inspiration, but *in terms of the Gnostic myth.*"[27] Bultmann has first established for himself the origin of the Fourth Gospel; and asserting that this Gospel has its roots in second-century Gnosticism, he then proceeds to show that a Gnostic redeemer myth permeates the passages referring to Jesus' origin.

In many ways, such an interpretation can sound convincing and gains many supporters. The question which must be faced, however, is this: Is there sufficient evidence to prove that John's Gospel relies upon

[24]*The Gospel According to John.* Grand Rapids: Eerdmans, 1971; p. 711.
[25]See C. H. Dodd, *Fourth Gospel*, p. 259.
[26]O. Cullmann, *Christology*, p. 298. Also see C. K. Barrett, *The Gospel According to St. John.* London: S.P.C.K., 1965; p. 288.
[27]R. Bultmann, *Gospel*, pp. 250f.

a Gnostic myth? The answer to this question is negative, especially since the time the Gospel of Thomas was discovered in the sands of Egypt and the Dead Sea Scrolls in the Judean desert.

It is one thing to say that a Gnostic myth circulated in pre-Christian form at the time the Fourth Gospel was written. It is another thing to prove it. Concludes Leon Morris, "So for all its popularity in some circles this idea must be discarded."[28] All indications are that though John was aware of Gnostic teachings, the Gnosticism we have come to know does not belong to the age of John. In his Gospel account, John does not present Gnostic ideas but Christian teachings. He presents Jesus Christ as the Son of God.

III. RESURRECTION

If any subject is a subject of debate, it is the New Testament teaching on the resurrection of Jesus. The theologian who wishes to say something significant on this subject goes to the very basis of Christianity. He cannot deny the resurrection of Christ and still call himself Christian. Paul in the middle of the first century said, "if Christ has not been raised, then our preaching is in vain and your faith is in vain" (I Cor. 15:14). This is the watershed. The Christian believes the resurrection of Christ, the unbeliever rejects this doctrine.

Issues

Should the teaching of Jesus' resurrection be simply a matter of believing or not believing, the whole subject would not claim the center of attention. However, it is a matter of interpretation. How does the modern theologian interpret the teaching of the resurrection?

In the Old Testament and in the New Testament, several people have returned from the state of death. Lazarus, for example, spent four days in the grave, but at the command of Jesus came back to life. All these people, however, came back to life in their ordinary every-day existence. They did not appear in a glorified state, and after some time elapsed they died again. The resurrection of Jesus, to be sure, was a permanent resurrection to life; his was a resurrection not to life in previous form, but to life in immortal glory and power. Jesus' resurrection is unique.

What kind of a resurrection did Jesus experience? In modern debate, the question is asked: did Jesus really rise from the dead? What do we know about his resurrection from the Gospel accounts? Nowhere in the New Testament do we find an eyewitness account of the resurrection, because those who were appointed to watch the grave of Jesus

---

[28]*Gospel,* p. 63.

became like dead men (Matt. 28:4). The evidence for the resurrection
hinges on the empty grave and the appearances of Jesus.

The modern contention is that the evangelists do not emphasize the
fact of the empty tomb. In Mark's account, attention is not drawn so
much to the empty grave as to the appearance of Jesus in Galilee.
The women are told. "Do not be amazed; you seek Jesus of Nazareth,
who was crucified. He has risen, he is not here; see the place where
they laid him. But go, tell his disciples and Peter that he is going before
you to Galilee: there you will see him, as he told you" (16:6, 7). Besides, in the early Christian church, the empty tomb was not used as an
argument supporting the event of Jesus' resurrection. Certainly, Paul
would have referred to the empty tomb in his great resurrection
chapter of his First Epistle to the Corinthians. But apart from the
Gospels, the expression does not occur. In fact, the word "tomb" is
only used in the four Gospels.[29]

Furthermore, Jesus' body experienced a fundamental change at the
time of the resurrection. Though his body appeared to be the same
because his disciples recognized him and saw the marks in his hands,
side, and feet, his body had changed. During his earthly ministry,
Jesus had taught his disciples and his questioners that the resurrection
implied a transformation of the body of man. In answer to a question
concerning the resurrection, Jesus answered the Sadducees, "but those
who are accounted worthy to attain to that age and to the resurrection
from the dead neither marry nor are given in marriage, for they cannot
die any more, because they are equal to angels and are sons of God,
being sons of the resurrection" (Luke 20:35f.). The resurrected body,
according to Jesus, differs from the mortal body. Life in the resurrected
state is on a different plane.

Paul explains the difference still further when he tells the Corinthian
believers in his first epistle that the resurrection of the body is not a
return to a physical body. "It is sown a physical body, it is raised a
spiritual body. If there is a physical body, there is also a spiritual body"
(15:44). A perishable physical body simply cannot inherit the kingdom
of God (v. 50).

Another contention is that the Easter narratives are not at all uniform.
Whereas the four evangelists follow a basic pattern in presenting the
passion narratives, they do not present a logical precise report of the
events which occurred on Easter and the following days and weeks.
Neither does the author of Acts, nor does Paul in I Corinthians 15.

In the account of Matthew, it appears that the women were present
when the angel of the Lord descended and rolled away the stone. So
were the guards, but they became like dead men (Matt. 28:2-4). The

---

[29]H. Anderson, *Jesus and Christian Origins.* New York: Oxford, 1964; pp. 194f.

question is asked why the women came to the grave with spices, knowing that a stone too heavy for them to move was placed before the
opening of the tomb. Furthermore, guards had been placed at the
grave; it was their duty to keep people away from the sealed sepulchre.
In the other Gospels, nothing is said about the guards. Because of
Matthew's information on the sealed tomb and the presence of the
guards, the question of the women reported by Mark is meaningless:
"Who will roll away the stone for us from the door of the tomb?"
(16:3).

According to Paul in his resurrection chapter, I Corinthians 15, Jesus
appeared to Peter, then to the twelve, then to over five hundred
brethren at one time, afterwards to James, next to all the apostles, and
last of all to Paul (vv. 5-8). Though the disciples said to the two men
of Emmaus, "The Lord is risen indeed, and has appeared to Simon"
(Luke 24:34), the Gospel accounts nowhere record that Jesus appeared
to Peter on Easter. "The one story which *a priori* one would have
expected to survive intact would be that of the Lord's appearance to
Peter. But it is not so. By the time of the writing of the gospels it had
disappeared leaving behind no more than an echo, and that not in
narrative but in credal form ('The Lord is risen indeed, and has appeared to Simon'), which Luke has some difficulty in attaching as an
awkward pendant to his Emmaus story."[30] Moreover, if the requirement
for apostleship was to be a witness to the resurrection, Paul qualifies
because of his vision on the way to Damascus. But there is no record
of Matthias.

And a last contention is that the faith of the early Christian community is more important than the fact of the resurrection. The Easter
stories, therefore, are not factual accounts of what happened; rather,
the fact of the resurrection is clothed in the language of faith. The
early Christian church confessed its faith and was not interested in
presenting an account of historical facts. It is the fact of faith, and not
the fact of the event. This is evident in the resurrection account of the
saints who were raised when Jesus died. Matthew says, "the tombs also
were opened, and many bodies of the saints who had fallen asleep
were raised, and coming out of the tombs after his resurrection they
went into the holy city and appeared to many (27:52f.). The context
indicates that an earthquake, at the time of Jesus' death, split the rocks
and opened the graves; the saints were raised, but they came out of
their tombs after Jesus' resurrection. Then they went into the holy city
and were seen by many. What did they do and why did they remain in
their tombs until Jesus arose from the grave? Joachim Jeremias points

---

[30]C. F. Evans, *Resurrection and the New Testament.* Naperville: Allenson, 1970; p.
53. Also see Jeremias, *New Testament Theology,* pp. 307f.

to this passage as proof that the resurrection meant the dawn of the new age; in the thinking of the disciples, "Jesus' resurrection was not an isolated event but was directly bound up with many resurrections."[31]

Interpretations

How does the modern theologian interpret the resurrection of Jesus? What does the post-Bultmannian say about this unique event? Does he regard the resurrection as such historical? Does the redaction critic say that Jesus bodily rose from the grave? Is faith in the physical resurrection openly confessed?

Well, the redaction critic is not vague at all in his interpretation of Jesus' resurrection. Hans Conzelmann, among others, contends that the resurrection cannot be proved as a historical event. "The element of event in the resurrection is rather to be characterized thus: faith understands the resurrection objectively as the prior element of the action of God, by understanding that it is founded precisely on this resurrection by God. Resurrection is thus visible only to faith and its truth cannot be proved historically."[32] The resurrection is recognized only in faith; when the gospel is proclaimed, the believer sees the Risen Lord.

Theologian Willi Marxsen has made a serious attempt in presenting his views on the resurrection of Jesus of Nazareth in language understandable to the listener who is not theologically schooled. Marxsen makes it clear that believing in the resurrection of Jesus of Nazareth does not differ at all from believing the teachings of the earthly Jesus. Because the teaching of Jesus is alive today and calls men to faith, the resurrection of Jesus is meaningful and relevant.

Of course, this approach evokes the question: How is the resurrection of Jesus understood? Marxsen argues that in the Christian church the theologian must be given the freedom to explore different interpretations. And as long as he believes in the teachings of Jesus, his faith in the resurrection will not be shaken or diminished by this or that interpretation. Faith in Jesus and his resurrection, therefore, must be seen apart from the mode of the resurrection. Marxsen puts it this way:

> One man says, "I believe, I am involved: Jesus is risen"; and he thinks of the original event in the following terms: Jesus was raised physically from the dead by God, and that fact makes it possible for me to believe in Jesus today.
> Another man says, "I believe, I am involved: Jesus is risen"; and he thinks of the original event as follows: Jesus' body remained in the grave; but Jesus was raised spiritually to new life, and that fact makes it possible for me to believe in Jesus today.

---

[31]New Testament Theology, p. 309.
[32]Outline, p. 68.

We can certainly be "involved" once we have been informed about a past event. But our involvement cannot determine whether the information itself is true, false, or inaccurate.... Consequently our present involvement, which we express in the words "Jesus is risen," is incapable of deciding anything about the mode of the resurrection.[33]

How does Marxsen interpret the resurrection accounts of the Gospel of Matthew? What does he do with the account in the Gospel of Mark or the Third Gospel? Marxsen points out that the Gospel of Matthew has no proper ending because the writer does not inform the reader what happened to Jesus, if we are asking Matthew to furnish the evidence for a historical account. Matthew does not provide this evidence because it is not his purpose. Instead, he wants to show the presence of Jesus to his disciples. Says Marxsen, "But, as if with outstretched arm, Jesus points his disciples forward after his death. Though physically he remains behind, he is experienced by his own as the *present* Lord to whom all authority has been given in heaven and on earth. As this Lord he is always with them."[34] It is, therefore, a matter of faith which carries the disciples through after the death of Jesus. Matthew does not focus attention on faith in the resurrection; rather, he indicates that faith in Jesus is all important for Jesus' followers. It is the faith which the disciples had when Jesus was still living which now continues, even though Jesus' life came to an end when he died.

Without doubt, when Marxsen says that Jesus remained behind physically, he does not believe that Jesus arose and left behind the empty grave. Jesus' death marks the end of his physical existence; the body of Jesus came to an end, but faith in Jesus continues. Yet Marxsen has something to say about the "stories of the empty tomb." In his opinion, Mark is the first to offer the reader a story about the empty tomb. Well, what does Mark do for the reader? He does not say that the women came to the tomb, found it empty, and then they concluded that Jesus arose. It is just the other way around. The young man at the grave, says Mark, told the women that Jesus of Nazareth had risen and was not in the tomb. Then he directed their attention to the empty grave. These women came to the grave with the message of the resurrection which they then and there interpreted visually. When this took place, concludes Marxsen, is difficult to say.

Marxsen asserts that in Jewish-Christian circles faith in Jesus was formulated in the form of a story: the story of an empty tomb. This story was told and retold and in the course of time changed in form and appearance. This is evident, contends Marxsen, in the Gospel of

---

[33]*The Resurrection of Jesus of Nazareth.* Philadelphia: Fortress, 1970; pp. 20, 21.
[34]*Ibid.,* p. 168.

Luke, in which the story of the empty tomb comes before that of the resurrection of Jesus. First Luke relates the story of the women going to the grave, where they did not find the body of Jesus, and then he tells his readers about the resurrection. Moreover, the story of the empty tomb differs considerably from that of Mark's Gospel, which is another indication that Luke wrote his Gospel in a time when the church had formulated its faith in Jesus.

Besides the question about the empty tomb, the question concerning the appearances of Jesus must be answered. Did not Jesus appear to many people as Paul indicates pointedly in the first part of his chapter on the resurrection (I Cor. 15:5-8)? But notice, says Marxsen, that Paul in listing the appearances of Jesus speaks of categories: "he appeared to Cephas, then to the twelve. Then he appeared to more than five hundred brethren at one time, most of whom are still alive, though some have fallen asleep. Then he appeared to James, then to all the apostles. Last of all, as to one untimely born, he appeared also to me." Peter (Cephas) is followed by the twelve, and James is followed by the apostles. Peter belongs to the twelve and he belongs to the apostles. The question arises whether Peter experienced three appearances.[35] But a question of greater significance is whether this information relates to that of the Gospels.

In the Gospels, Peter takes priority because he is frequently addressed by Jesus and is designated to give leadership. It is Peter, therefore, who leads others to faith in Jesus. Hence, Paul is able to write that Jesus appeared to Peter, then to the twelve. That means, Peter is the one who leads the twelve to faith. Who are these twelve? The Gospels indicate that after the death of Judas, there are only eleven disciples of Jesus. Marxsen thinks that "the twelve" are a group of people, distinct from the apostles, who are probably the bearers of the Jesus tradition. They are missionaries, led by Peter. James is mentioned because he is the leader of the church at Jerusalem, who stands at the head of many people — a group of some five hundred brethren. "We can now go on to ask: why are we told that all these different groups experienced an appearance of Jesus? What is the point of the narrative? I think it is this: their faith, the manifold functions which they exercised, are all in the ultimate resort based on the first appearance to Peter. They are all summed up in this appearance."[36] Marxsen, however, does not want to imply that there was only one appearance; there may have been more, such as the special appearance to Paul. But the point is that Peter because of his faith in Jesus led others to faith; and when the others came to believe Jesus, they began their missionary

---

[35]*Ibid.*, p. 81.
[36]*Ibid.*, p. 92.

task by bringing still others to a faith in Jesus. Seeing Jesus in faith prompts a believer, therefore, to be a witness of his resurrection. Thus, James, as leader of the Jerusalem church, was instrumental in leading more than five hundred people to believe in Jesus.

Marxsen is still faced with the question when Peter had this vision of Jesus. To his credit, he does answer this question. The time when Peter had a vision of Jesus was in Galilee. After Jesus' death on the cross, the disciples left Jerusalem and returned to Galilee. They went back to their former occupation, fishing. There on the Galilean lake, Peter saw that Jesus was calling him to be a fisher of men. It was at this time that Peter understood this direct saying of Jesus. Peter believed the word of the earthly Jesus and his faith established him in his calling. Thus, the words of Jesus spoken before Good Friday became meaningful to Peter when he was fishing on the lake after Jesus' death. Jesus, so to speak, met with Peter after his crucifixion and death, and told him to carry out what he had commanded Peter during his life on earth. And Peter, by faith, began to understand the full implication of these words. So did the other disciples. In short, "we must understand that the disciples, having found faith after Good Friday, acquired *insight* as to who Jesus was and now *see* him like this as well. They are therefore depicting a reality, though, of course, not a historical reality. Anyone who looks for *direct* history in these images has simply failed to grasp their character."[37]

One thing which Marxsen advises his readers to do is to examine the stories of the resurrection very carefully. However, when he himself examines these stories, he enumerates so many apparent discrepancies that he indirectly, if not directly, discredits the record set forth by the individual evangelists. He deliberately sets out to cut the tie between history and faith; while removing the historical foundation of the doctrine of the resurrection, Marxsen places all the emphasis on faith. In order to accomplish this, he has to jump to a number of unjustified conclusions which lack the support of careful exegesis.

Let us begin with the subject of the empty tomb. Why would the evangelists present all the details of the women buying spices, of the women going to the grave at daybreak, of an earthquake, of the appearance of angels, and of the fear and astonishment coming upon the women so that they trembled? Why would the evangelists mention all these details if the women were fully acquainted with the doctrine of the resurrection? Why would they tremble and be afraid if they came to the tomb with the message of the resurrection? And why does Mark add that after the women had fled from the grave, "they said nothing

[37]*Ibid.,* p. 160.

to any one"? If they were fully acquainted with the message of the resurrection formulated by the early Christian community, they would proclaim the message to everyone. We would expect that these women — to follow the reasoning of Marxsen — were missionaries seizing every opportunity to lead others to faith in Jesus. They would be the last to be silent.

Perhaps the very fact that the subject of the empty tomb crops up repeatedly in Marxsen's presentation may be seen as an indication that he is unable to put the matter to rest. The echo of the empty tomb is a reverberating sound which Marxsen simply cannot silence.

Though the appearances of Jesus are discussed at great length, Marxsen argues that these were visions captured in the minds of men like Peter and Paul. If this were true, why would Peter preach in the house of Cornelius, the centurion stationed in Caesarea that God raised Jesus on the third day and made him manifest? Why would he add that Jesus did not appear to all the people, "but to us who were chosen by God as witnesses, who ate and drank with him after he rose from the dead" (Acts 10:41)? Certainly these words do not fit a pre-Easter situation at all. Besides, the reference to eating and drinking is to post-Easter scenes vividly described by Luke and John. Luke records that Jesus ate a piece of broiled fish in the evening of resurrection day in the presence of the disciples (Luke 24:42f.), and John relates the incident of Peter's restoration after Jesus had breakfast with the disciples on the shore of the Galilean lake (John 21:12ff.). Would Peter distort the facts when preaching to a God-fearing Cornelius? To say that the early Christian community formulated and fashioned these accounts is unwarranted. Unquestionably, a basic trustworthiness is evident in these recorded events, especially when Luke, in his preface, states that he has followed all things accurately concerning the things which have been accomplished (1:1-4). And a writer must be taken at his word unless he can be proven wrong by indisputable evidence. Marxsen fails to present this evidence.

Furthermore, Marxsen may readily refer to the words of Paul, "if Christ has not been raised, then our preaching is in vain and your faith is vain" (I Cor. 15:14). He may contend that he believes these words to be true, that with his interpretation of the resurrection of Jesus these words still stand and are applicable, and that his faith in Jesus is not in vain. But the fact remains that Paul in this resurrection chapter is not speaking about a subjective vision which he had of Jesus; instead, he outlines the implications of Jesus' resurrection for the bodily resurrection of the believers. Paul is stressing the reality of the physical resurrection of Jesus in relation to the physical resurrection of those that belong to Christ. Why would Paul write that Christ is raised from the dead as the first fruits, and afterwards at Christ's coming those that belong to him? Why would he spell out in detail the resurrection of the believer? He writes, "We shall not all sleep, but we shall all be changed, in a moment, in the twinkling of an eye, at the last trumpet. For the trumpet will sound, and the dead will be raised imperishable, and we shall be changed" (15:51f.). Certainly, Paul would not have devoted the lengthiest chapter of First Corinthians to the doctrine of the resurrection if he wished to say that man's resurrection is equivalent to his conversion experience.

In the thinking of Marxsen, the resurrection of Jesus seems to be a mere interpretation and nothing more. In fact, he is not so much interested in the resurrection of Jesus as such. He rather stresses the faith of the individual believer who is in touch with the living Jesus. But by doing this, Marxsen has reduced the Easter event of Jesus' resurrection to nothing more than an idea. This is not only unwarranted; it constitutes a break with and departure from the *Christian* faith which is founded on the unambiguous teaching of the physical resurrection of Jesus of Nazareth.

Modification

Wolfhart Pannenberg, a contemporary German theologian, has voiced serious objections against the teaching which presents the resurrection of Jesus as an idea rather than a historical fact. He writes, "The importance of the question of whether or not Jesus really rose from the dead should be clear enough. But how can it be answered? Could the answer be left to a mere decision of faith? This must be absolutely denied."[38]

He views the resurrection of Jesus not as an act of bringing a body back to life, comparable to a person arising from sleep, but rather as a transformation. He refers to I Corinthians 15:50, 53. "I tell you this, brethren: flesh and blood cannot inherit the kingdom of God, nor does the perishable inherit the imperishable. . . . For this perishable nature must put on the imperishable, and this mortal nature put on immortality."

What happened in Jerusalem? Did Jesus appear to the disciples? Was the tomb empty? Pannenberg thinks that the appearances of Jesus and the women discovering the empty tomb are events which happened independently. These events were connected only when the traditions of the appearances and the empty tomb began to develop. These Easter events are proof that they in themselves constitute historical reality.

---

[38]"Did Jesus really rise from the dead?" *New Testament Issues,* ed. R. Batey, New York and Evanston: Harper & Row; p. 103.

How does Pannenberg understand the historicity of the resurrection? He gives this summary of his views: "We saw that something happened in which the disciples in these appearances were confronted with a reality which also in our language cannot be expressed in any other way than by that symbolical and metaphorical expression of the hope beyond death, the resurrection from the dead. Please understand me correctly: Only the *name* we give to this event is symbolic, metaphorical, but not the reality of the event itself. The latter is so absolutely unique that we have no other name for this than the metaphorical expression of the apocalyptical expectation. In this sense, the resurrection of Jesus is an historical event, an event that really happened at that time."[39]

All this is a definite affirmation of what the Christian church has always proclaimed, except that the event of the resurrection has never been described as metaphorical and symbolic. Is a reference to Paul's resurrection chapter and an explanation that Jesus' body was not revived but transformed sufficient reason to call the event metaphorical? What do the individual Gospel writers say about the resurrection of Jesus? Do they portray the event as something which must be understood metaphorically?

Though the approach of Pannenberg differs from that of Bultmann and Marxsen, the use of symbolism with respect to the name of the resurrection event does raise the question how he understands the Biblical reports. The fact that he elaborates on Paul's vision of Jesus and Paul's interpretation of the resurrection is indicative of Pannenberg's view of the Biblical reports of the Easter events. He openly states that the reports on the resurrection in the Gospels are legendary which hardly contain a historical kernel of their own.[40] If then Pannenberg discredits the historicity of the resurrection accounts in the Gospels, what does he do with the appearances of Jesus in the forty-day period between Easter and Ascension, and what does he do with the reports concerning the empty tomb?

When he writes about the appearances of Jesus, Pannenberg puts everything in the context of Paul's experience on the way to Damascus. But he hesitates to say something about the appearances of Jesus mentioned in the Gospels and those listed by Paul in I Corinthians 15. Yet he does affirm that the appearances of the resurrected Jesus came from heaven. They differ only from Paul's Damascus experience in regard to the light flashing from heaven. That means that the resurrected Jesus never appeared physically and that his appearances were experi-

39*Ibid.*, p. 115. Also see his "The Revelation of God in Jesus of Nazareth" *New Frontiers in Theology*, Volume III, *Theology and History*, editors, J. M. Robinson and J. B. Cobb, Jr. New York and Evanston: Harper & Row, 1967; p. 115.
40*Jesus—God and Man*, Philadelphia: Westminster, 1968; p. 89.

enced in the form of visions. Although these visions were not subjective experiences but objective experiences, Pannenberg refrains from affirming the Biblical teaching that Jesus arose physically. For this reason, he has chosen to designate the event of the resurrection as metaphorical. The resurrection of Jesus is symbolical because it was ascertained only in the way Paul saw Jesus when he was converted on the way to Damascus. The resurrection is therefore only an objective vision experienced by those to whom Jesus appeared. Concisely, there is no physical resurrection from the grave.

At this juncture, Pannenberg cannot ignore the tradition concerning the empty tomb. He affirms the historicity of this tradition, but this does not mean that he affirms the Biblical reports of this event. Whereas the Gospel writers state that the women found the grave empty in the early hours of Easter morning, Pannenberg describes the factuality of the empty grave as follows: "Jesus' empty tomb, if it should be a historical fact, belongs to the singularity of Jesus' fate. He precisely had not lain many years in his grave or decayed as the other dead had, but after a short time he was 'transformed' to another life, whatever such an expression may mean."[41] The tradition of the empty grave is able to stand by itself. The crux of the matter, however, is the physical resurrection of Jesus. And precisely on this point, Pannenberg retreats in a sphere of uncertainty. For him, Jesus' body was transformed to another life; yet he is not sure what such a statement implies. He has rejected the Biblical accounts recorded in the Gospels because he fails to find a kernel of historical truth in them. Obviously, because he has rejected the Scriptural accounts, he has to rely upon his own insight as to what happened at Easter. Therefore, Pannenberg expresses uncertainty and wishes to call the resurrection event symbolical or metaphorical. However, "the meaning and interpretation of the resurrection does not depend on our understanding of it but on the revelation of its meaning in the New Testament."[42]

Conclusion

A few points stand out when the flood of theological discourse begins to recede. And these points can be summarized rather briefly: they concern the physical resurrection of Jesus, the appearances of Jesus, the subject of the empty tomb, and the apparent discrepancies in the Gospel records.

Despite the differences of opinion which modern theologians may voice, they seem to be unanimous in their denial of the physical resur-

---

[41]*Ibid.*, p. 100.
[42]J. C. DeYoung "Event and Interpretation of the Resurrection" *Interpreting God's Word Today,* ed. S. Kistemaker, Grand Rapids: Baker, 1970; p. 144.

rection of Jesus. They assert with one accord that the Gospel record simply does not present a historically accurate picture. Only by reading Paul's interpretation of the resurrection can they gain certainty. "These authors develop their position on the basis of several observations. In the first place, they note that the appearances all involve believers or people who as a result become believers. Furthermore, they occurred to an early community that lived in expectation of the rule of God in light of the life of Jesus. As a consequence, it is the fact of the Easter faith with which we must primarily deal, not the fact of the resurrection."[43] That is, even though the one theologian may stress history more than the other, as long as he considers the content of the resurrection accounts in the Gospel legendary, he severs the tie between history and faith. The basis for faith, consequently, is shifted. Faith is no longer rooted in the historical reality of the Easter event; it must be found in the experiences of the first believers, who communally and individually formulated their confessions. When the relation of historical event and faith is cut, faith is no longer based on historical fact but on the fact of Easter faith. In a word or two, it is faith based on faith.

Furthermore, when modern theologians write about the appearances of Jesus, they place them in the framework of Paul's experience when he saw Jesus. This vision of Paul on the way to Damascus is interpreted by the modern theologian either as a subjective experience (Marxsen) or an objective confrontation (Pannenberg). Though Marxsen wishes to go on record that he simply does not know with certainty what happened to Paul on the way to Damascus, he intimates that Paul was familiar with the Christian proclamation which on that journey overwhelmed him. Persecutor became preacher because of the power of the message. Hence, the vision of Paul was entirely subjective: he meditated on the spoken word which he had consistently rejected, but which he on the road to Damascus accepted. Then he "saw" Jesus.

Pannenberg rejects the subjective experience hypothesis. Instead, he exegetes the Scripture passages which speak of Paul's conversion; and he concludes that Paul while journeying to Damascus must have seen Jesus in a spiritual body. He explains Paul's experience, therefore, as an objective confrontation. This is correct, for Paul himself writing his first letter to the Corinthians asks, "Am I not free? Am I not an apostle? Have I not seen Jesus our Lord?" (9:1). But when in that same epistle, Paul mentions the people who also have seen Jesus, Pannenberg has no right to assume that all these people listed in 15:5-7 had exactly the same experience as Paul, except for the light phenomenon. Pannenberg fails to deal with the appearances of Jesus in the period between Easter and Ascension. He does not speak without hesitation and reserve about

---

[43]C. C. Anderson, *Critical Quests of Jesus*. Grand Rapids: Eerdmans, 1969; p. 194.

the bodily appearances of the resurrected Jesus. Even though Pannenberg stresses the historicity of the resurrection, he demurs when the
historicity of Jesus' appearances in the forty-day period preceding the
Ascension calls for his affirmation. C. F. Evans makes this telling remark, "Thus it has been justly observed that he speaks a great deal
more, and a great deal more confidently, about the resurrection in
general than about the resurrection of Jesus in particular."[44]

It is one thing to speak with confidence about the resurrection with
the help of the New Testament epistles; it is another thing to speak
about the resurrection of Jesus in the light of the testimonies of eyewitnesses and ministers of the word (Luke 1:2). It is one thing to
write without reserve about the vision which Paul had on the road to
Damascus; it is another thing to write, in the same vein, about the
physical appearances of Jesus to those people mentioned by Paul in
I Corinthians 15. The exegete must note the fact that these people
precede Paul and that their experiences occurred before Paul set out for
Damascus. If their accounts of Jesus' appearances are older than Paul's
vision, the exegete is confronted with questions pertaining to chronology.
That is, he must return to the sources, written in order that we may
believe (John 20:31).

The sources indicate that the word of the eyewitnesses is to be taken
seriously because they saw the body of Jesus, which had been placed
in the tomb. "In this light, we think it biblically irresponsible to claim
that Christian faith in the resurrection is independent of the question
of whether or not Jesus lies buried in Palestine — Christian faith in the
resurrection is in continuity with apostolic faith in the resurrection, and
there is no evidence that the first witnesses took such a stance of in-
difference toward the body in the tomb."[45] The basis for knowledge of
the resurrection does not lie in man's suppositions; on the contrary, it is
found in the Gospel accounts.

But the Gospels and the Acts together with the list of appearances in
I Corinthians 15 do not lend themselves for reconstructing a chronologi-
cal sequence of the events which took place between Easter and Pente-
cost. An attempt to harmonize the factual information might give the
following sequence: the women went to the tomb in the early hours of
Easter morning, saw the stone rolled away, talked to the angels, re-
turned to Jerusalem and met Jesus; they told the disciples, whereupon
Peter and John rushed to the tomb; in the meantime, Jesus appeared to
Mary Magdalene, who had stayed behind in the garden; Peter and
John saw the burial clothes of Jesus and returned to Jerusalem believing;

[44]*Resurrection*, p. 180.
[45]R. E. Brown, "The Resurrection of Jesus." *The Jerome Biblical Commentary*, ed.
R. E. Brown, *et al.*, Englewood Cliffs, N.J.: Prentice-Hall, 1968; Vol. II, p. 792.

also to Peter Jesus appeared that day. In the evening of that day, Jesus appeared first to the two men of Emmaus, and then to the disciples without Thomas. One week later, he appeared to them again when Thomas was present, too. Afterwards, Jesus appeared to seven disciples along the shore of the Galilean lake; later, on a mountain in Galilee, he appeared to the eleven disciples; and last but not least, Jesus appeared to the disciples in Jerusalem before he ascended. And somewhere in that forty-day period he appeared to James.

Yet no attempt to present somewhat of a sequence is made by the evangelists. Not even Paul presents an accurate chronology. Why does the one evangelist report appearances of Jesus in Galilee and the other in Jerusalem? Reinier Schippers, commenting on the localities of the appearances, observes that the individual evangelist was guided by his purpose and goals. Matthew, describing the beginning of Jesus' ministry, places "Galilee of the nations" in a prominent light. It is Galilee where Jesus is preaching the Sermon on the Mount. Therefore, Matthew concludes his Gospel account with the appearance of Jesus on a mountain in Galilee. In Galilee, the apostles receive the Great Commission, to make disciples of all nations. Luke, on the other hand, begins his Gospel with a description of Zechariah in the temple of Jerusalem. As can be expected, Luke also ends his Gospel with the reference to the temple at Jerusalem to which the disciples returned after the ascension of Jesus.[46] Considering, therefore, the purpose of the individual evangelist, we may assert that the Gospel writers did not attempt to present an accurate and complete account of the Easter and post-Easter events. No attempt is made by Paul either to present an accurate list of names and places of Jesus' appearances. The reason may very well be that Paul is only interested in mentioning some of the traditions which circulated in the early church. He mentions the names of people who have seen Jesus. And a reference to these names would be sufficient to the early church because they represented the apostolic witnesses honored by the church. The testimony of the apostolic witnesses was sufficient.

When we read the Gospel records, the book of Acts, and Paul's Epistles with a view to their individual purpose and goal, many of the so-called discrepancies disappear. We should not expect from these writers that which they did not intend to give. In their accounts they present the irrefutable evidence that Jesus arose physically from the grave. They express the mystery of the Christian religion in the words of an ancient hymn recorded in I Timothy 3:16,

> He was manifested in the flesh,
> vindicated in the Spirit,

---

[46] "De Opstanding van Jezus van Nazareth in het Nieuwe Testament." *Gereformeerd Theologisch Tijdschrift,* 68 (1, 1968); p. 53.

seen by angels,
preached among the nations,
believed on in the world,
taken up in glory.

8. INTERPRETATION

"What does Scripture say?" This question is usually asked when a point of doctrine is discussed and when a definitive answer is needed. Even though the Bible is consulted and the necessary information is obtained, the discussion may continue because of the interpretation of a particular passage in Scripture. That is, a passage of Scripture quoted to support a doctrinal point of view may be interpreted in more than one way. No student of the Bible comes to the text without presuppositions, without instruction, without commitment. And because of these variations in thinking and training, differences in interpreting Scripture arise.

General principles, of course, are universally accepted and applied. They enunciate the believer's approach to Scripture and consist of the acknowledgement that Scripture reveals all things needed for the believer's salvation, and that it is the believer's rule of faith and life. Moreover, because of the commitment to let Scripture be its own interpreter, a Christian does not need theological training in order to interpret the Bible. Through the Spirit Scripture itself conveys to the believer the knowledge he needs for salvation. No help from man is necessary to come to such knowledge.

Nevertheless, problems remain in interpreting the Bible, because every believer approaches Scripture with his own inclinations and interests. By way of illustration, numerous people view Niagara Falls every day. The painter is inspired to put his artistic talent to work and portray the view on canvas. The engineer looks at the rushing water and thinks of possibilities to harness the falls for the production of energy. And the geologist, viewing the structure of the rocks, wonders how long the falls will last. Each one considers Niagara Falls from his own perspective and interest. Likewise, scholars view Scripture from various perspectives. One may have an interest in the history the Bible presents; another may focus his attention on its teachings.

Existentialist Approach

A modern theologian approaches Scripture with a particular question in mind. He wants to know what a given text means for him today. This is the existentialist approach initiated by the New Testament theologian Rudolf Bultmann (1884–1976). In Bultmann's view the language of the New Testament conveys first-century concepts of the universe, the world of demons and supernatural manifestations. First-century believers described the universe as a three-level structure made up of heaven, earth, and underworld. Mental illness was attributed to demons who took possession of man's mind, and supernatural events in connection with the birth, life, death, resurrection, and ascension of Jesus were expressed symbolically and incorporated in confessional statements. Bultmann held that the mythological language of these confessional statements had to be reinterpreted, not eliminated. "The real purpose of myth is not to present an objective picture of the world as it is, but to express man's understanding of himself in the world in which he lives. Myth should be interpreted not cosmologically, but anthropologically, or better still, existentially."[1]

Bultmann wanted to make the message of the New Testament text relevant to modern man. He reinterpreted the Bible and, in doing so, disregarded the historical setting of the individual Gospel passages. Bultmann had, in effect, cut the tie with history.

Post-Bultmannian Approach

Ernst Fuchs (1903–) and Gerhard Ebeling (1912–) developed an approach to Scripture that differed slightly from that of Bultmann. They asked how the New Testament could become the living word of God, so that it could be heard anew. The implication is that the written Word no longer communicates, for mere repetition of the text of the New Testament in the ears of today's listener may convey a message which differs from what the text actually means. The words which we read in the New Testament text are not our words, for they do not belong to our world and thinking.[2] The task of the theologian is to translate the truth embodied in the text of the New Testament into words that convey this truth meaningfully to man today.

What is at stake, therefore, is not the text itself but the truth which the text conveys. The interpreter is to translate the truth expressed in the New Testament text into a message meaningful for man today. The interpreter must develop an understanding of the person who was

---

[1] R. Bultmann, "New Testament and Mythology," *Kerygma and Myth* (Editor, H. W. Bartsch), London: SPCK, 1972; p. 10.

[2] G. Ebeling, *Word and Faith*, Philadelphia: Fortress, 1963. E. Fuchs, *Hermeneutik*, Tübingen: J.C.B. Mohr, 1970.

originally addressed by the New Testament text, combined with an understanding of modern man. It is no secret that in order to be able to do this the interpreter ought to be fully acquainted with, and an articulate expositor of, existential philosophy.[3] Before he can understand the New Testament, he must be an existential philosopher.

The post-Bultmannian is not so much concerned with hermeneutics as with a set of rules. Ebeling stated that "hermeneutics as the theory of understanding must therefore be the theory of words."[4] This approach to the New Testament text is based on a linguistic theory which is centered on the interpreter. The exegete decides how the truth of the text must be translated, and he subjectively interprets without regard to grammar, history, and theology. For example, the resurrection of Jesus ought not to be seen as only an event in history. The believer's faith in the resurrection (I Cor. 15:14) does not rest on historical fact. It rests on hearing the proclamation of faith. Therefore, say the followers of Bultmann, even Paul had received his information by way of those who preached faith in the resurrection. Obviously, when the subjective self is allowed to get at the truth of the New Testament text by disregarding its historical setting and its theological implications, the interpreter can make the text say something which differs completely from its original meaning. The exegete, therefore, has put something into the text instead of drawing the meaning from the text.

The Bultmannian interpreter has departed from the Reformation adage that says, *fides quae creditur*, that is, the faith or the teaching which is believed. The objective stance of regarding the basic doctrine of Scripture as foundational has been replaced by *fides qua creditur*, that is, the subjective faith by which man believes. In short, the interpreter has shifted his emphasis from the basic objective teaching of Scripture to a subjective belief of the individual. The foundation of the Christian's faith has been replaced with something that is entirely subjective and changeable.

Structuralism

In recent years another school of thought, known by the name *structuralism*, has emerged. Though the concept of structuralism finds its origin in the movement created by Ferdinand de Saussure (1857–1913) and Claude Levi-Strauss (1908–), only in the last decade has it been discussed in the English-speaking world. Structuralism has to do with language and related areas of interest. When it applies to language, it is known as structural linguistics. At times the structuralists work out an analysis of basic oppositions. These may be spatial: the earth versus

---

[3]J. D. Smart, *The Interpretation of Scripture*, Philadelphia: Westminster, 1961; p. 49.
[4]Ebeling, p. 319.

the sky and land versus sea. In respect to New Testament research, for example, the opposition is between John the Baptist and Jesus Christ. John and Jesus are portrayed as heroes; nevertheless they are opposites. Already at the time of conception, the contrast is clear. John's mother is past child-bearing age; Jesus' mother is a virgin. John is a descendant of the priestly line of Aaron; Jesus is of the royal house of David. John lives in the desert; Jesus in towns and cities. At the time of their death, they reverse roles. That is, John dies a royal death in a king's palace; Jesus is crucified outside the city as a criminal. John dies when the king Herod celebrates a birthday; Jesus dies when the nation Israel celebrates the Passover.[5]

The structural analyst does not intend to provide a study in contrasts, for this has been done by other students of the New Testament. Rather, he uses the contrasts to illustrate the universal structure of myth, which is considered to be devoid of history. History for the structuralist is completely irrelevant. Whether something happened in a historical context really does not matter, says the structuralist, because the message of myth and not the historical context is important.

The structuralist does not ask what the writer of the passage wants to convey. The structuralist is only interested in the linguistic elements and their relationships. This excessive concern with linguistics results in a rather one-sided exposition of the text.

Moreover, the structuralist is justifiably criticized for his disregard for the historical setting of a New Testament passage. An exegete cannot afford to delete the historical situation which the text describes. If he deliberately neglects this aspect of the text, he runs the risk of distorting its meaning and doing an injustice to its intention.

Structuralism may have its place, but only when as a discipline it takes on a full-orbed hermeneutical method of interpreting a text in its totality. A text must be seen in relation to its context, its literary characteristics, its historical background, and its theological implications. Only when the interpreter does full justice to the text by applying this hermeneutical method can structuralism make a worthy contribution.

Whenever historical and theological considerations are slighted, interpreters of the text apply limited hermeneutical rules. Even when all the rules are observed, the emphasis may be placed on one particular rule at the expense of the rest. Exponents of the new hermeneutic as well as those adhering to structuralism interpret Scripture in such a way that history all but disappears from the scene.

---

[5]E. Leach, "Structuralism and Anthropology," *Structuralism: An Introduction* (Editor, D. Robey), Oxford: Clarendon, 1973; pp. 53-55. Also see A. C. Thiselton, "Keeping up with Recent Studies. II. Structuralism and Biblical Studies: Method or Ideology?" *Expository Times* 89 (1977-78); p. 332. V. Poythress, "Structuralism and Biblical Studies," *Journal of the Evangelical Theological Society* 21 (1978); pp. 221-237. D. A. Carson, "Hermeneutics: A Brief Assessment of Some Recent Trends," *Themelios* 5 (1980); pp. 12-20.

Comprehensive Approach

Studies in the structure and composition of an individual Gospel prove to be rewarding and give the reader insight into the thinking of the writer. Guided by the Holy Spirit in composing the Gospel, the author nevertheless developed his own structure, though his Gospel always remains an account of the life and teachings of Jesus Christ.

Herman Ridderbos has traced the structure of the Gospel according to Matthew in terms of proportion and content.[6] He sees the First Gospel as an architectonic structure which shows harmony and purpose. Moreover, he views Matthew's Gospel from a structural redaction perspective. Thus, the Gospel has a total of 1,070 verses which divide rather conveniently into four equal parts of about 270 verses each.

A. 1:1–9:35. Jesus' birth; his appearance in Israel; his miracles of healing (270 verses).

B. 9:36–16:12. Jesus' teaching ministry; his confrontation with Israel (270 verses).

C. 16:13–23:39. Announcement of his death; the way to the cross (272 verses).

D. 24:1–28:20. Farewell; suffering, death, and resurrection (258 verses).[7]

Part A (1:1–9:35) can be divided into two sections of 90 and 180 verses each, and Part B (9:36–16:12) into two sections of 180 verses and 90 verses each. A pattern of A.B.–B.A. is evident. The writer of the First Gospel displays architectural skills in constructing his gospel. For example, the 90 verses in the first section of Part A (1:1–4:25) compose the introduction to the entire Gospel. The next 180 verses cover the Sermon on the Mount (5:1–7:29) and the miracles of healing performed by Jesus (8:1–9:35). The first section of Part B presents the teaching ministry of Jesus (9:36–13:52) in 180 verses; and the last section of Part B displays in 90 verses Jesus' confrontation with Israel (13:53–16:12).

Jesus Christ is portrayed as the Savior of Jew and Gentile. Already in the genealogy (1:1–17), Gentile women are mentioned among Jesus' ancestors. In the next chapter, Matthew relates that wise men from the East came to Jerusalem and asked, "Where is he who has been born king of the Jews?" (2:2). Presenting the healing miracles of Jesus (8:1–4), Matthew first records the incident of the Jewish leper who was cleansed and, in accordance with Jewish law, sent to the priest. The next healing miracle concerns the healing of a centurion's servant on the strength of the faith of the Gentile centurion (8:5–13). Matthew

---

[6]H. Ridderbos, *Studies in Scripture and Its Authority*, St. Catharines: Paideia, 1978; pp. 47-55.
[7]Ridderbos, p. 48.

arranges his material to focus attention on the Christ who is the Savior of both Jew and Gentile.

Matthew anchors his Gospel in the redemptive history of the life, death, and resurrection of Jesus Christ, the son of Mary and Son of God. In his account, Matthew presents the theological message of Jesus fulfilling the Old Testament prophecies concerning the promised Messiah. Matthew presents the Gospel of Christ.

Principles

The New Testament has been written in a context and a culture which is no longer ours. For the interpreter of Scripture it is well to make a thorough study of the cultural setting of the times in which Jesus and the apostles lived. He needs to become acquainted with the customs, traditions, and religious observances of the Jew and Gentile of that day. For example, in order to gain a clear understanding of Jesus' conversation with the Samaritan woman at Jacob's well near Sychar (John 4:5–29), the exegete must learn why the woman came alone to the well in the heat of the day, why Jesus talked to the woman, and why the Samaritans worshiped at Mount Gerizim in Samaria.

Closely connected with the cultural principles is the historical principle. The student of Scripture must acquire an understanding of the times in which an incident occurs or is recorded. For example, Jesus' reference to the man of noble birth who went to a distant country to have himself appointed king (Luke 19:12) is an obvious reference to Herod Archelaus (Matt. 2:22), who journeyed to Rome after the death of his father, Herod the Great, to petition Emperor Augustus to appoint him king. The exegete should know that Archelaus had killed some 3,000 Jews celebrating the Passover at Jerusalem before he left for Rome. And last, the interpreter should place these historical facts in the context of Jesus' approach to Jerusalem just days before the annual celebration of the Passover feast.

A third principle of interpretation is the theological one. This principle should not be contrasted to the historical and cultural rules of exegesis, but should be seen as an integral complement. The theological principle stresses the unity of the Old and New Testaments. It gives expression to the maxim taught by St. Augustine:

> The New is in the Old concealed;
> The Old is in the New revealed.

The numerous citations from the Old Testament in the Gospel of Matthew are an eloquent testimony to the unity of Scripture. Both Old and New Testaments are essential components of God's revelation to sinful man. As he applies the theological principle to the two parts of Scripture, the interpreter ought to be guided by these considerations:

The Old Testament offers the key to the right interpretation of the New. The New Testament is a commentary on the Old.[8]

The student of Scripture should ask what the evangelist's theological purpose was for writing the Gospel. John spells this out in the twentieth chapter of his account by saying that he wrote "that you may believe that Jesus is the Christ, the Son of God, and that believing you may have life in his name" (v. 31). Theologically, John stresses the divinity of Jesus, though in his presentation he does not in the least minimize Jesus' humanity. Especially in the discourses, John refers to the divine nature of Jesus and his heavenly descent.

A fourth principle is the one which touches on the text, the grammar, and the literary form of a given passage in the New Testament. The exegete must ascertain that the text in hand is the best available. For the student of the Bible this means that he needs to know something about the various translations of the Bible. He must not be satisfied with a translation unless he is sure that it closely follows the original autographs. With the help of grammar books, lexicons, dictionaries, concordances, and various translations of the Bible, he is in a position to determine the exact reading of the text. The interpreter, nevertheless, must face the interesting nuances of a word. For example, the word *woman* in the account of Jesus' conversation with the Samaritan woman at the well, recorded in John 4, has a somewhat derogatory connotation. Though the translation "lady" or "girl" would be a perfectly correct equivalent for the Greek word for woman (*gunē*),[9] the translator is guided by the context. The word is woman. Yet when Mary informs Jesus that the supply of wine had been used up at the wedding feast in Cana, Jesus addresses her with the word *woman* (John 2:4). In view of the context, the address does not imply a derogatory meaning; rather it conveys endearment and respect. One translation renders Jesus' remark as follows: "Dear woman, why do you involve me?" (NIV). A translator, therefore, must be guided not merely by a lexicon and concordance but also by the context in which a word or phrase is used. In this respect, let Scripture be its own interpreter.

Method

Teaching the skill of exegesis is not confined to giving the student a few hermeneutical principles. Merely applying these principles does not always guarantee satisfactory results. The interpreter must become fully involved in the meaning of the text. The advice of the eighteenth-century Lutheran theologian Johann A. Bengel is still applicable today: "Apply your whole self to the text, and the whole text to yourself."

---

[8]L. Berkhof, *Principles of Biblical Interpretation*, Grand Rapids: Baker, 1978; p. 137.
[9]I. H. Marshall, *New Testament Interpretation*, Grand Rapids: Eerdmans, 1977; p. 12.

The following procedure for a biblico-theological interpretation of a New Testament text will be helpful to the exegete.

1. Define the limits of the text and focus attention on the perimeter of the passage.
2. Read the text in both the immediate and the broad context. The immediate context includes the paragraph and the chapter in which the text is located. The broad context includes the book in which the text is located as well as other books written by the same writer. In addition, look at the text in the light of Scripture and let the light of Scripture shine on the text. That is, view the whole of Scripture from the perspective of the text, and view the text from the perspective of the whole of Scripture.
3. Analyze the text grammatically. Using lexicons and dictionaries, translate the text as accurately as possible. Consult grammar books, diagram sentences to determine the basic relationship of words, and check textual variants in the text and footnotes.
4. Study the meaning of key words and phrases in their immediate context. The wording of parallel passages and the meaning of synonyms should be compared and contrasted. The use of word-study books and concordances is a rewarding exercise in gaining a greater understanding of the text.
5. Pay attention to the literary characteristics of the text, the structure and style. Determine whether the text is poetry, dialogue, parable, theological reflection, or concluding remarks. Literary characteristics have a definite bearing on the interpretation of the text.
6. Make a thorough study of the historical setting of the text. For example, an interpretation of Jesus' conversation with the woman at the well (John 4) demands a thorough investigation of the origin, history, religion, and customs of the Samaritans. The interpreter must understand the cultural setting in which the incident took place.
7. Consider the theological connection the text has with the Old Testament. That is, discover whether the passage is a quotation from, or an allusion or reference to, the Old Testament. Consult books on Biblical Theology.
8. Check exegetical and theological commentaries on the text. It is advisable to consult at least four different commentaries in order to become acquainted with insights and emphases of individual commentators.
9. Seek to determine the one unifying theme of the passage and construct a subservient outline. The central message of the text should be expressed naturally and exegetically in all the parts of the outline.

Ask the question: "Do I present Christ?" Jesus Christ must be central to the message of the text.

10. Apply the text to the needs of today. This is not always easy to do. Yet the interpreter faces the question, "How do I apply the text today?" For instance, what is the significance of the parable of the Good Samaritan? Along the Jericho road of human life lie many of the world's unfortunates. The command "Go and do likewise" is just as relevant today as it was in the day when Jesus addressed the theologian who heard the story first.

Expound the Scriptures
Exhort the sinner
Exalt the Savior

BIBLIOGRAPHY

Abbott, E. A. *Correction of Mark*. London, 1901.

Abel, E. L. "Who Wrote Matthew?" *New Testament Studies* 17 (1971): 2.

Anderson, Charles C. *Critical Quests of Jesus*. Grand Rapids: Wm. B. Eerdmans, 1969.

—— *The Historical Jesus: A Continuing Quest*. Grand Rapids: Wm. B. Eerdmans, 1972.

Anderson, Hugh. *Jesus and Christian Origins: A Commentary on Modern Viewpoints*. New York: Oxford University Press, 1964.

Baird, J. Arthur. *Audience Criticism and the Historical Jesus*. Philadelphia: Westminster Press, 1969.

Barbour, R. S., "Recent Study of the Gospel According to St. Mark." *Expository Times* 79 (1968):11

Barclay, William. *The First Three Gospels*. Philadelphia: Westminster Press, 1967.

Barrett, Charles K. *The Gospel According to St. John*. London: S.P.C.K., 1965.

—— *The Gospel According to St. John*. Rev. ed. Philadelphia: Westminster Press, 1978.

—— *Luke the Historian in Recent Study*. Philadelphia: Fortress Press, 1970.

Beegle, Dewey M. *God's Word into English*. Rev. ed. Grand Rapids: Wm. B. Eerdmans, 1964.

Berkeley Version. Grand Rapids: Zondervan Publishing House, 1965.

Berkhof, Louis. *Principles of Biblical Interpretation*. Grand Rapids: Baker Book House, 1950.

Black, Matthew. *The Scrolls and Christian Origins*. New York: Charles Scribner's Sons, 1969.

Bornkamm, Gunther. *Jesus of Nazareth*. Translated by Irene and Fraser McLuskey. New York: Harper & Row Publishers, 1960.

Bornkamm, Gunther, G. Barth, and H. J. Held. *Tradition and Interpretation in Matthew*. Philadelphia: Westminster Press, 1963.

Brown, Raymond E. *The Anchor Bible: The Gospel According to John* (i-xii). Garden City, NY: Doubleday & Company, 1966.

—— "The Gospel of Thomas and St. John's Gospel." *New Testament Studies* 9 (1962-63).

Raymond E. Brown et. al., eds. "The Resurrection of Jesus." *The Jerome Biblical Commentary*. Vol. 2. Englewood Cliffs, NJ: Prentice-Hall, 1968.

Brownlee, William H. *The Meaning of the Qumran Scrolls for the Bible*. New York: Oxford University Press, 1964.

Bruce, F. F. *The New Testament Documents: Are They Reliable?* 5th ed. reprint. Grand Rapids: Wm. B. Eerdmans, 1967.

Bultmann, Rudolf. *The History of the Synoptic Tradition*. New York: Harper & Row Publishers, 1963.

_____*Jesus Christ and Mythology*. New York: Charles Scribner's Sons, 1958.

_____*Jesus and the Word*. New York: Charles Scribner's Sons, 1958.

_____*The Gospel of John*. Philadelphia: Westminster Press, 1971.

_____"New Testament and Mythology." *Kerygma and Myth*. Edited by H. W. Bartsch. London: SPCK, 1972.

_____*Primitive Christianity in Its Contemporary Setting*. New York: Meridian, 1946.

_____*Theology of the New Testament*. Vol. 1. New York: Charles Scribner's Sons, 1952.

_____*Theology*. Vol. 2. New York: Charles Scribner's Sons, 1955.

Butler, B. C. *The Originality of Matthew*. Cambridge: University Press, 1951.

Cadbury, Henry J. *The Making of Luke-Acts*. London: S.P.C.K., 1961.

Carson, D. A. "Hermeneutics: A Brief Assessment of Some Recent Trends." *Themelios* 5 (1980):2.

Chapman, J. *Matthew, Mark, and Luke*. London, 1937.

Clark, K. W. "The Manuscripts of the Greek New Testament." *New Testament Manuscript Studies*. Chicago: University of Chicago Press, 1950.

Colpe, C. "Son of Man." *Theol. Wörterbuch Zum N.T.* Vol. 8. Stuttgart: Kohlhammer, 1969.

Conzelmann, Hans. *The Theology of St. Luke*. Translated by Geoffrey Buswell. New York: Harper & Row Publishers, 1961.

_____*An Outline of the Theology of the New Testament*. Translated by John Bowden. New York: Harper & Row Publishers, 1969.

Cullmann, Oscar. *The Christology of the New Testament*. Philadelphia: Westminster Press, 1959.

Danielou, Jean. *The Dead Sea Scrolls and Primitive Christianity*. Baltimore: Helicon Press, 1958.

De Young, J. C. "Event and Interpretation of the Resurrection." In *Interpreting God's Word Today*, edited by Simon J. Kistemaker. Grand Rapids: Baker Book House, 1970.

Dibelius, Martin. *From Tradition to Gospel*. London: Nicholson & Watson, 1934.

Dodd, C. H. *The Apostolic Preaching and Its Developments*. 1936. Reprint. Grand Rapids: Baker Book House, 1980.

_____*The Interpretation of the Fourth Gospel*. New York: Cambridge University Press, 1953.

Drane, J. *Jesus and the Four Gospels*. New York: Harper and Row Publishers, 1979.

Dungan, D. L. "Mark—The Abridgement of Matthew and Luke." *Perspective* 11 (1970):1-2.

Ebeling, Gerhard. *Word and Faith*. Philadelphia: Fortress Press, 1963.

Edwards, Richard A. *A Theology of Q: Eschatology, Prophecy, Wisdom*. Philadelphia: Fortress Press, 1976.

Eusebius. *Ecclesiastical History*. Loeb Classical Library, vol. I. New York: G. P. Putnam's Sons, 1926.

Evans, C. F. *Resurrection and the New Testament*. Naperville, IL: Allenson, 1970.

Farmer, William R. *The Synoptic Problem*. New York: Macmillan, 1964.

Fuchs, E. *Hermeneutik*, Tübingen: J.C.B. Mohr, 1970.

Gardner-Smith, P. *St. John and the Synoptic Gospels*. Cambridge: University Press, 1938.

Gartner, B. *The Theology of the Gospel of Thomas*. New York: Harper & Row Publishers, 1961.

Gaster, Theodor H. *The Scriptures of the Dead Sea Sect*. London: Secker & Warburg, 1957.

Gerhardsson. *Memory and Manuscript*. Lund: Gleerup; and Copenhagen: Munksgaard, 1961.

Gilkes, A. N. *The Impact of the Dead Sea Scrolls*. London: Macmillan, 1962.

Goodspeed, Edgar J. *Matthew, Apostle and Evangelist*. New York: Holt, Rinehart & Winston, 1959.

Goulder, Michael D. *Midrash and Lection in Matthew*. London: S.P.C.K., 1974.

Grant, Robert M. *The Secret Sayings of Jesus*. New York: Doubleday & Company, 1960.

Gundry, R. H. *The Use of the Old Testament in St. Matthew's Gospel*. Leiden: Brill, 1967.

Guthrie, Donald. *The Gospels and Acts: New Testament Introduction*. Downers Grove, IL: InterVarsity Press, 1964.

Haenchen. *Die Apostelgeschichte*. Göttingen: Vandenhoeck & Ruprecht, 1956.

Hare, D. R. *The Theme of Jewish Persecution of Christians in the Gospel According to St. Matthew*. Cambridge: University Press, 1967.

Harrison, Everett F. "Gemeindetheologie: The Bane of Gospel Criticism." In *Jesus of Nazareth: Saviour and Lord*, edited by Carl F. H. Henry. Grand Rapids: Wm. B. Eerdmans, 1966.

Heard, R. *An Introduction to the New Testament*. New York: Harper & Row Publishers, 1950.

Hendriksen, William. *New Testament Commentary: Exposition of the Gospel According to John*. Grand Rapids: Baker Book House, 1953.

——— *Exposition of the Gospel According to Luke*. Grand Rapids: Baker Book House, 1978.

——— *Exposition of the Gospel According to Mark*. Grand Rapids: Baker Book House, 1975.

——— *Exposition of the Gospel According to Matthew*. Grand Rapids: Baker Book House, 1973.

Hennecke, Edgar. *New Testament Apocrypha*. Vol I. Philadelphia: Westminster Press, 1959.

Hooker, Morna D. *The Son of Man in Mark*. London: S.P.C.K., 1967.

Hunter, Archibald M. *Introducing the New Testament*. London: SCM, 1961.
_____ *According to John: The New Look at the Fourth Gospel*. Philadelphia: Westminster Press, 1968.

Irenaeus. *Adv. Haer: The Ante-Nicene Fathers*. Grand Rapids: Wm. B. Eerdmans, 1962.

Jeremias, Joachim. *New Testament Theology*. New York: Charles Scribner's Sons, 1971.
_____ *The Prayers of Jesus*. Naperville, IL: Allenson, 1967.

Käsemann, Ernst. *Essays on New Testament Themes*. London: SCM, 1964.
Kilpatrick, George D. *The Origins of the Gospel According to St. Matthew*. New York: Oxford University Press, 1946.
Kistemaker, Simon J. *The Psalm Citations in the Epistle to the Hebrews*. Amsterdam: Van Soest, 1961.
Klijn, A. F. *An Introduction to the New Testament*. Leiden: Brill, 1967.
Klooster, Fred. *Quest for the Historical Jesus*. Grand Rapids: Baker Book House, 1977.
Knigge, H. D. "The Meaning of Mark." *Expository Times* 80 (1969):12.
Kummel, Werner G. *The Theology of the New Testament*. Nashville: Abingdon Press, 1973.

Ladd, George E. *The Young Church: Acts of the Apostles*. Nashville: Abingdon Press, 1964.
_____ *The New Testament and Criticism*. Grand Rapids: Wm. B. Eerdmans, 1967.
_____ *A Theology of the New Testament*. Grand Rapids: Wm. B. Eerdmans, 1974.
Lane, W. L. *The Gospel According to Mark*. Grand Rapids: Wm. B. Eerdmans, 1974.
Leach, Edmund. "Structuralism and Anthropology." In *Structuralism: An Introduction*, edited by D. Robey. Oxford: University Press, 1973.
Lightfoot, Joseph B. *The Apostolic Fathers*. Grand Rapids: Baker Book House, 1962.
Lightfoot, R. H. *St. John's Gospel*. Oxford: University Press, 1960.

Mansoor, Menahem. *The Dead Sea Scrolls*. Grand Rapids: Wm. B. Eerdmans, 1964.
Maier, Gerhard. *The End of the Historical-Critical Method*. St. Louis: Concordia Publishing House, 1977.
Marshall, I. Howard. *Luke: Historian and Theologian*. Grand Rapids: Zondervan Publishing House, 1971.
_____ *I Believe in the Historical Jesus*. Grand Rapids: Wm. B. Eerdmans, 1977.
_____ *New Testament Interpretation: Essays in Principles and Methods*. Grand Rapids: Wm. B. Eerdmans, 1977.
_____ *The Gospel of Luke: A Commentary on the Greek Text*. Grand Rapids: Wm. B. Eerdmans, 1978.
_____ "Recent Study of the Gospel According to St. Luke." *Expository Times* 80 (1968):1.

_____ "Recent Study of the Acts of the Apostles." *Expository Times* 80 (1969):10.
_____ "The Son of Man in Contemporary Debate." *Evangelical Quarterly* 42 (1970):2.
_____ "The Synoptic Son of Man Sayings in Recent Discussion." *New Testament Studies* 12 (1966):4.
Martin, R. P. "The Life-setting of Mark." *Expository Times* 80 (1969):12.
_____ *Mark: Evangelist and Theologian*. Grand Rapids: Zondervan Publishing House, 1973.
_____ "St. Matthew in Recent Study." *Expository Times* 80 (1969):5.
Marxsen, Willi. *Mark the Evangelist*. Translated by Roy A. Harrisville. Nashville: Abingdon Press, 1969.
_____ *The Resurrection of Jesus of Nazareth*. Philadelphia: Fortress Press, 1970.
Metzger, Bruce M. *The New Testament: Its Background, Growth, and Content*. Nashville: Abingdon, 1965.
_____ *The Text of the New Testament*. New York and London: Oxford University Press, 1964.
Meyer, B. F., *The Aims of Jesus*. London: SCM, 1979.
Meyer, M., ed. *The Nag Hammadi Library in English*. New York and San Francisco: Harper and Row Publishers, 1977.
Morris, Leon. *The Gospel According to John*. Grand Rapids: Wm. B. Eerdmans, 1971.
_____ *Studies in the Fourth Gospel*. Grand Rapids: Wm. B. Eerdmans, 1969.
Murphy, R. E., *The Dead Sea Scrolls and the Bible*. Westminster, MD: Newman Press, 1963.

Pannenberg, Wolfhart. "Did Jesus Really Rise from the Dead?" In *New Testament Issues*, edited by R. Batey. New York and Evanston: Harper & Row Publishers, 1970.
_____ *Jesus: God and Man*. Philadelphia: Westminster Press, 1968.
_____ "The Revelation of God in Jesus of Nazareth." In *New Frontiers in Theology*. Vol. III, *Theology and History*. Edited by J. M. Robinson and J. B. Cobb, New York and Evanston: Harper & Row Publishers, 1967.
Perrin, Norman. *Jesus and the Language of the Kingdom*. Philadelphia: Fortress Press, 1976.
_____ *What Is Redaction Criticism?* Philadelphia: Fortress Press, 1969.
Petrie, C. Stewart. "The Authorship of 'The Gospel According to Matthew': A Reconsideration of the External Evidence." *New Testament Studies* 14 (1967):14.
_____ "Q Is What You Make It." *Novum Testamentum* 3 (1959).
Pinnock, Clark H. *Biblical Revelation—The Foundation of Christian Theology*. Chicago: Moody Press, 1971.
Poythress, V. "Structuralism and Biblical Studies." *Journal of the Evangelical Theological Society* 21 (1978).

Quispel, G. "L'Evangile selon Thomas et le Diatessaron." *Vigiliae Christianae* 13 (1959).

Revised Standard Version. Cleveland and New York: World Publishing Company, 1962.

Ridderbos, Herman N. *Studies in Scripture and Its Authority*. Hauppauge, NY: Paideia, 1978.
Riesenfeld, H. "The Gospel Tradition and Its Beginnings." *Studia Evangelica*. Berlin: Akademie, 1959.
Robertson, Archibald T. *A Harmony of the Gospels*. New York: Harper & Row Publishers, 1922.
Robinson, James M., editor. *New Frontiers in Theology*. Vol. 1, *The New Hermeneutic*. New York: Harper & Row Publishers, 1964.
_____ *A New Quest of the Historical Jesus*. London: SCM, 1959.
Rohde, Joachim. *Rediscovering the Teaching of the Evangelists*. Philadelphia: Westminster Press, 1968.
Ross, Alexander. *The Epistles of James and John*. Grand Rapids: Wm. B. Eerdmans, 1954.

Schippers, R. "De Opstanding van Jezus van Nazareth in het Nieuwe Testament." *Gereformeerd Theologisch Tijdschrift* 68 (1968):1.
_____ "Pre-Synoptic Tradition in I Thessalonians 2:13-16." *Novum Testamentum* 8 (1966):2-4.
Schmidt, K. L. *Der Rahmen der Geschichte Jesu*. Berlin: Trowitzch, 1919.
Schurer, Emil. *A History of the Jewish People in the Time of Jesus Christ*. Division II, Vol. I. Edinburgh: T. & T. Clark, 1885.
Schweizer, Eduard. *The Good News According to Mark*. Richmond: John Knox Press, 1970.
Smalley, S. S. "The Johannine Son of Man Sayings." *New Testament Studies* 15 (1969):3.
_____ *John: Evangelist and Interpreter*. Exeter: Paternoster, 1978.
Smith, D. M. *The Composition and Order of the Fourth Gospel*. New Haven and London: Yale University Press, 1965.
Stauffer, Ethelbert. *New Testament Theology*. London: SCM, 1955.
Stein, Robert. *The Method and Message of Jesus' Teaching*. Philadelphia: Westminster Press, 1978.
Stendahl, Krister. *The School of St. Matthew and Its Use of the Testament*. Philadelphia: Fortress Press, 1968.
Stonehouse, Ned B. *The Witness of the Synoptic Gospels to Christ*. Reprint. 1 vol. combining *The Witness of Matthew and Mark to Christ* and *The Witness of Luke to Christ*. Grand Rapids: Baker Book House, 1979.

Taylor, Vincent. *The Gospels*. 11th ed. London: Epworth Press, 1967.
Thiselton, Anthony C. "Keeping Up with Recent Studies, II; Structuralism and Biblical Studies: Method or Ideology?" *Expository Times* 89 (1977-78).
Tödt, Heinz E. *The Son of Man in the Synoptic Tradition*. Philadelphia: Westminster Press, 1965.

Westcott, B. F. *The Gospel According to St. John*. Reprint. Grand Rapids: Baker Book House, 1980.
_____ *Some Lessons on the Revised Version of the New Testament*. 4th ed. London, 1903.
Wilson, Robert Mcl. *Studies in the Gospel of Thomas*. London: Mowbray, 1960.

Zuntz, Guenther. *The Text of the Epistles*. New York: Oxford University Press, 1953.

INDEX OF NAMES

INDEX OF TEXTS